HOAXED!

Media Failures in the Field of Cryptozoology

MICHAEL NEWTON

Typeset by Jonathan Downes, and Saskia England
Cover and Layout by SPiderKaT for CFZ Communications
Using Microsoft Word 2000, Microsoft Publisher 2000, Adobe Photoshop CS.

First published in Great Britain by CFZ Press

CFZ Press
Myrtle Cottage
Woolsery
Bideford
North Devon
EX39 5QR

ISBN: 978-1-909488-16-8

For Ken Gerhard

Table of Contents

Introduction

R eporters love a scandal. Most will never break a story on the scale of Watergate, or even Martha Stewart's inside-trading felonies. They must content themselves with local peccadilloes—and if they can have a laugh at someone else's personal embarrassment along the way, so much the better. Sometimes it is easier to take an "exposé" delivered by some third party and run with it than to perform the normal function of a journalist.

Sometimes they simply get it wrong.

Cryptozoology has always been a discipline beset by error, simple-minded pranks, and outright fraud. Honest mistakes are easiest to understand—a bear, briefly glimpsed in presumed Bigfoot territory; a manatee mistaken for a mermaid, and so on. Bernard Heuvelmans, the "Father of Cryptozoology," compiled a list of 587 alleged sea-serpent sightings logged between 1639 and 1966, dismissing 52 as sightings of large animals well known to science (whales, giant squids and basking sharks, etc.) logged by frightened or ignorant witnesses.[1] Some of the errors, it must be admitted, are both more original and more amusing.

> * In January 1921, townsfolk from Logan, Ohio, rallied to defend their town against a giant snake, reported hissing in the nearby woods. After shotgun blasts dispatched the "monster," it was found to be a 40-foot length of hose, abandoned five years earlier by sawmill operator Jesse Thompson. A colony of bees inside the hose provided its sinister sound track.[2]

> * In 1926, Scottish embryologist, member of Parliament, and future Governor General of Canada, John Graham Kerr described a giant prehistoric viper, *Bothrodon pridii,* based on his examination of a supposed fossil fang, 2.5 inches long, found in the Gran Chaco wilderness of South America. Years later, the "fang" was correctly identified as a prong broken off the shell of a large marine snail, the Chiragra spider conch (*Harpago chiragra*).[3]

> * Since 1891, several witnesses have claimed encounters with a kind of Scottish

Bigfoot, dubbed the Big Grey Man of Ben Macdhui (a peak in the Cairngorm Mountains of the eastern Highlands). Investigation suggests that the creature may be a "Brocken spectre"—that is, an observer's own shadow, cast upon the upper surfaces of clouds opposite the sun and thus made to appear enormous.[4]

* For generations, natives of New Ireland and Papua New Guinea regaled visitors with stories of a merbeing variously known as *ri, ilkai,* or *pishmeri.* In February 1985, members of an expedition sponsored by the Ecosophical Research Association observed and photographed three specimens, positively identifying the *ri* as an ordinary dugong (*Dugong dugon*).[5]

* In December 2003, villagers on the Indonesian island of Java announced the capture of a python measuring 50 feet in length, weighing 985 pounds. When examined by a British herpetologist in early January, the snake—dubbed "Fragrant Flower" by its captors—shrank precipitously, to an estimated 21 feet and some 220 pounds.[6]

Deliberate hoaxes are something else entirely. Author Chad Arment identifies three broad categories of fraud in the field of cryptozoology: (1) pranks targeting innocent parties, who then report the incidents to others in good faith; (2) hoaxers fabricating evidence in a direct attempt to fool investigators; and (3) the simple telling of a tale, with no attempt to stage a scene or offer any evidence.[7]

Arment includes among the latter category various "traveler's tales" and hoaxed newspaper articles frequently printed as "silly season" filler during the 19th and early 20th centuries. One obvious example, published by an Ohio newspaper on 28 July 1871, described the panic inspired by a 15-foot snake that "has already swallowed an old gray horse, a lot of children, and a mowing machine."[8]

Another, which in fact bamboozled serious researchers for decades, was reported on 4 July 1884, by British Columbia's *Daily Colonist,* announcing the capture an ape-like creature nicknamed "Jacko," which allegedly was held in jail and viewed by hundreds of curious spectators. Venerable Sasquatch researcher John Green exposed Jacko as a newspaper hoax in January 1975, yet seemed to hedge his bets three years later, in his book *Sasquatch: The Apes Among Us,* by including the account of one Chilco Choate, who claimed his grandfather was present at the creature's capture. As late as 1983, British archaeologist Myra Shackley reported Jacko's capture as "confirmed" by witness August Castle—who, by his own admission to John Green, never saw the creature.[9]

Examples of Arment's first category, innocent dupes deceived by pranksters, would include a "giant snake" report from Montreal, Québec, in August 1938. Investigators found that two mischievous lads had rigged strings to a fire hose, dragging it around a flooded quarry in a bid to frighten a night watchman. That same year, likely inspired by news of the Canadian hoax, firemen in Green Bay, Wisconsin, used one of their own hoses to fake "python" sightings.[10]

The most pernicious crypto-hoaxes, whether perpetrated for profit or simple amusement, involve fabrication of physical evidence. Such fakes may be patently obvious, such as the "sea-serpent" fashioned from a tree trunk for a photo staged at Ballard, Washington, in 1906.[11] Others are more perplexing.

A case in point comes from Decatur, Illinois. There, in spring of 1962, author Loren Coleman writes: "I[,] along with my brothers William and Jerry, came upon an ape-like footprint in a dry creek bed....The print was about 10 inches long, with a clearly visible large opposed toe, the hallux, sticking out to the right of a left foot impression." Coleman attributes the footprint to a creature he calls a North American ape—"Nape," for short.[12] The track was photographed, but captions accompanying published versions of the photo describe it as a "reconstruction" prepared by one Zack Clothier from Coleman's original snapshot.[13]

Jerry Coleman tells a very different story of the track's discovery. In his version, he and five friends found the simian print, then rushed home to fetch brother Loren. The track was then "saved, photographed, measured and logged," before a more extensive search began. Only later, according to Jerry, did one of his playmates confess to faking the footprint. As Jerry explained it, "either Kenny [Manship] or Dave [Nichols] discovered a right boot print at the bottom of the gorge. The print had a thick stick the size and shape of a large thumb positioned on the right side. This stick had already been walked on by the original maker and one of the boys then pushed the stick down a little more on the far edge, thus making it appear as an ape's toe. Then, quickly chucking the stick and flipping out some of the dried top layer, he yelled at the other boys to see his 'great find.'"[14]

On 31 March 1972 a strange carcass was dragged from the chill waters of Scotland's Loch Ness. By a stroke of apparent good fortune, scientists from Yorkshire's Flamingo Park Zoo were on hand, having joined members of the Loch Ness Phenomena Bureau for an experiment using "hormone sex bait" to attract the lake's resident cryptid. Now, with a carcass in hand, zoo director Don Robinson told reporters, "I've always been skeptical about the Loch Ness Monster, but this is definitely a monster, no doubt about that. From the reports I've had, no one has ever seen anything like it before...a fishy, scaly body with a massive head and big protruding teeth." The find made global headlines the next morning—April Fool's Day—then provoked a high-speed chase as zoo staffers sought to abscond with the corpse, pursued by Fifeshire County police bent on enforcing a 1933 statute that bans removal of "unidentified creatures" from Loch Ness. Detained at Dunfermline, the Nessie-nappers surrendered their catch for examination by Michael Rushton, general curator of the Edinburgh Zoo, who quickly identified it as a male southern elephant seal (*Mirounga leonina*), native to the South Atlantic. John Shields, the Flamingo Park Zoo's education officer, soon confessed that the seal had been captured near the Falkland Islands, died shortly after its arrival in England, and was then employed in a practical joke.[15]

Thirty-three years later, in March 2005, two American tourists at Loch Ness allegedly found a deer's carcass at lakeside, with a large tooth or fang protruding from its flesh. As they told the tale, a passing game warden confiscated the tooth, but not before they photographed it, posting the photos online while clamoring for the return of their trophy. Zoologists viewing the photos soon identified their subject as the antler of a small deer, and the episode was subsequently revealed as a publicity stunt for author Steve Alten's new horror novel, *The Loch*. In the process of debunking the "Nessie tooth," reporters created a conundrum of their own, reporting that the antler belonged to "a roe muntjac deer."[16] In fact, the roe deer and muntjac belong to different genera, *Capreolus* and *Muntiacus,* respectively.

On 9 July 2008 Georgia residents Rick Dyer and Matthew Whitton posted a video to YouTube, claiming that they had discovered and preserved a Sasquatch corpse. Longtime researcher Carmine "Tom" Biscardi—embarrassed three years earlier, when his promise to air footage of a live Bigfoot through a pay-per-view webcam service proved false—joined Dyer and Whitton in proclaiming the creature's authenticity. "Last weekend," he told reporters, "I touched it, I measured its feet, I felt its intestines." He also promised DNA evidence, while allegedly paying Dyer and Whitton $50,000 for exclusive rights to their story. By August the fable unraveled, and the "specimen" was revealed as a Halloween-type costume frozen in a block of ice. Declaring himself an innocent dupe—the same explanation advanced for the prior hoax, in 2005—Biscardi announced plans to sue and recover his money. Dyer, meanwhile, was dismissed from his job as a deputy sheriff on charges of fraud.[17]

Our list of crypto-hoaxes could go on, but these examples make the point. The public obviously has an interest in discovering objective truth. Reporters serve a useful function when they clarify honest mistakes, and all the more so when they lampoon frauds and hypocrites. At other times, through eagerness to break a "scoop" or simple negligence, they drop the ball.

In recent decades, certain journalists have made a habit of accepting without question or investigation almost any claim pretending to debunk a famous cryptid sighting. Typically, the story comes from a purported hoaxer—an admitted liar, in effect—"confessing" long after the fact, and lacking any semblance of substantive proof. Often, the "exposé" evolves to contradict itself, but those repeating it don't seem to notice.

Or they just don't care.

The work in hand is not a brief for the existence of specific cryptids. Rather, it surveys the failure of selected authors—or the media in general—to question stories that are dubious at best, or plainly fraudulent at worst. Some may be classified as honest efforts to resolve enduring mysteries; others are shameless frauds: hoaxed hoaxes, if you will. Some critics refer to the self-styled "skeptics" and "critical thinkers" promoting such transparent fables as *skofftics*.

Hoaxed! consists of six topical chapters. Chapter 1 examines the media's treatment of a possible giant cephalopod beached near St. Augustine, Florida, in 1896. Chapter 2 considers efforts to debunk an alleged photograph of "Champ"—a supposed cryptid inhabitant of Lake Champlain—reportedly taken in 1977. Chapter 3 reviews claims that a local prankster faked large three-toed footprints found along Florida's Gulf Coast in 1948. Chapter 4 dissects assertions made by relatives of confessed Sasquatch hoaxer Raymond Wallace that he "invented" Bigfoot and that the cryptid "died" with him in 2002. Chapter 5 charts years of hoax claims leveled at a possible film of Bigfoot taken by Roger Patterson in California, in 1967. Chapter 6 probes assertions that the famous "surgeon's photo" of the Loch Ness Monster was faked in 1934.

You are the jury. When the evidence is laid before you, let the chips fall where they may.

References

1. Bernard Heuvelmans, *In the Wake of the Sea-Serpents* (New York: Hill and Wang, 1968), pp. 575-85.
2. Chad Arment, *Boss Snakes* (Landisville, PA: Coachwhip Publications, 2008), p. 19.
3. George Eberhart, *Mysterious Creatures* (Santa Barbara, CA: ABC-CLIO, 2002), p. 67.
4. Ibid., p. 51.
5. Ibid., p. 459.
6. "50-foot python caught in Indonesia," United Press International, 23 December 2003; John Aglionby, "Stay Still, Will You?" *The Guardian* (London), 4 January 2004.
7. Chad Arment, *Cryptozoology: Science & Speculation* (Landisville, PA: Coachwhip Publications, 2004), p. 15.
8. Arment, *Boss Snakes,* p. 239.
9. John Green and Sabrina Sanderson, "Alas, Poor Jacko," *Pursuit* 8:1 (January 1975): 18-19; John Green, *Sasquatch: The Apes Among Us* (Vancouver, BC: Hancock House, 1978), pp. 83-8; Myra Shackley, *Still Living?* (New York: Thames and Hudson, 1983), pp. 35-6.
10. Arment, *Boss Snakes,* pp. 12-14, 18.
11. "Pacific Sea Monster," The Museum of Hoaxes, http://www.museumofhoaxes.com/hoax/photo_database/image/pacific_sea_monster.
12. Loren Coleman, *Mysterious America* (New York: Paraview Press, 2001), p. 214.
13. Eberhart, p. 391.
14. Jerry Coleman, *Strange Highways* (Alton, IL: Whitechapel Productions, 2003), pp. 15-17.
15. "The Body of Nessie Found," The Museum of Hoaxes, http://www.museumofhoaxes.com/hoax/af_database/permalink/the_body_of_nessie_found.
16. "The Loch Ness Tooth," The Museum of Hoaxes, http://www.museumofhoaxes.com/hoax/archive/permalink/the_loch_ness_tooth.
17. "Bigfoot discovery revealed as rubber gorilla suit hoax," *The Telegraph* (London), 20 August 2008; "Searching for Bigfoot group to sue Georgia hoaxers," *Atlanta Journal-Constitution,* 20 August 2008.

1.
Octopus Giganteus

Dr. Webb's What-is-It

Anastasia Island lies along the northeast coast of Florida, its eighteen-mile length separated from the mainland by the Matanzas River—in fact, a saltwater estuary. Its lighthouse, once a watchtower for Spanish settlers fearing attack by Britain or France, dates from 1824. Part of the island lies within St. Augustine's city limits; its other modern settlements include St. Augustine Beach, Butler Beach, Crescent Beach, Anastasia and Coquina Gables.

On 30 November 1896 a strange visitor planted itself on St. Augustine Beach. Young bicyclists Herbert Coles and Dunham Coretter were first to spot the object, partially buried in sand. Believing it to be a whale's carcass, they rushed to notify Dr. DeWitt Webb, a local physician, amateur naturalist, and founder of the St. Augustine Historical Society and Institute of Science. Webb viewed the carcass on 1 December, observing the apparent stumps of arms and thereupon deciding that the pinkish-white object was a monstrous octopus. As described in the *New York Herald* on 2 December, "Its body, which is estimated to weigh about five tons, has sunk into the sand to a considerable depth, but that portion above the surface measures twenty-three feet in length, four feet in height, and more than eighteen feet across the widest part of its back."[1]

Inclement weather prevented further examination of the carcass until 5 December. Two days later, Webb returned with photographers, who snapped several exposures of the carcass. Another local, John L. Wilson, undertook private excavation around the remains, reporting exposure of tentacle fragments. As he told Webb, "One arm was lying west of the body, twenty-three feet long; one stump of an arm, west of the body, about four feet; three arms lying south of the body and from appearance attached to same (although I did not dig quite to body, as it lay well down in the sand, and I was very tired), longest measured over thirty-two feet, the other arms were three to five feet shorter."[2]

Sadly, Wilson worked alone, but his description was corroborated by South Beach hotelier George Grant, who penned a letter to his hometown newspaper, the *Pennsylvania Grit,* in Williamsport. Published on 13 December, it read:

"The head is as large as an ordinary flour barrel, and has the shape of a sea lion head. The neck, if the creature may be said to have a neck, is of the same diameter as the body. The mouth is on the under side of the head and is protected by two tentacle tubes about eight inches in diameter and about 30 feet long. These tubes resemble an elephant's trunk and obviously were used to clutch in a sucker like fashion any object within their reach. Another tube or tentacle of the same dimensions stands out on the top of the head. Two others, one on each side, protrude from beyond the monster's neck, and extend fully 15 feet along the body and beyond the tail. The tail, which is separated and jagged with cutting points for several feet, is flanked with two more tentacles of the same dimensions as the others and 30 feet long. The eyes are under the back of the mouth instead of over it. This specimen is so badly cut up by sharks and sawfish that only the stumps of the tentacles remain, but pieces of them were found strewn for some distance on the beach, showing that the animal had a fierce battle with its foes before it was disabled and beached by the surf." [3]

Dr. Webb, meanwhile, had sent his photos of the carcass to Joel Asaph Allen, at Harvard University's Museum of Comparative Zoology. Allen never responded, but Webb's letter and photographs somehow found their way to Yale professor Addison Emery Verrill, widely regarded as America's top malacologist (the study of mollusks).[4] Impressed, Verrill wrote a hasty article for the January 1897 issue of the *American Journal of Science,* which read in part: "The proportions indicate that this might have been a squid-like form, and not an Octopus. The 'breadth' is evidently that of the softened and collapsed body, and would represent an actual maximum diameter in life of at least 7 feet and a probable weight of 4 or 5 tons for the body and head. These dimensions are decidedly larger than those of any of the well-authenticated Newfoundland specimens. It is perhaps a species of Architeuthis. "[5]

The ink was barely dry on that article before Verrill changed his mind, in a piece written for the *New York Herald's* Sunday supplement of 3 January 1897. There, Verrill declared, "Dr. Webb has sent me photographs, four different pictures of the animal. They were taken on the same day he examined it. They show that the body is flattened, pear shaped, largest near the back end, which is broadly rounded and without fins. This form of the body and its proportions show that it is an eight-arm cuttlefish, or octopus, and not a ten-armed squid like the devil fish of other regions. No such gigantic octopus has been heretofore discovered."[6]

A storm swept the carcass back out to sea on 9 January, but it reappeared at Crescent Beach, two miles south of its original location, on 15 January. Dr. Webb's first effort to secure it failed, a gang of workmen finding themselves unable to shift the carcass bare-handed, but a team of horses finally succeeded in dragging the hulk farther inland, where it was photographed once more. A local tabloid newspaper, *The Tatler,* told its readers: "So far as can be determined at present, it belongs to no family not extinct, and is principally interesting on account of its great size, being about twenty-one feet long, without a head. Professor W. H. Dall of the Smithsonian Institute [*sic*], and Professor A. E. Verrill or Yale, are naturally much interested, and may be prevailed upon to visit."[7]

In fact, Webb had written to Dall—then curator of mollusks at the Smithsonian—urging him to "come down at once," but Dall's superiors denied him funds for travel. Neither would they pay to have the carcass shipped from Florida to Washington, D.C. Verrill likewise declined to make the journey from Connecticut. Taking rejection in stride, Webb cut several chunks from the globster for both malacologists.[8] His next letter to Dall, penned on 5 February 1897, read:

I made another excursion to the invertebrate and brought away specimens for you and for Dr. Verrill at Yale. I cut two pieces of the mantle and two pieces from the body and have put them in a solution of formalin for a few days before I send them to you. Although strange as it may seem to you, I could have packed them in salt and sent them to you at once although the creature has been lying on the beach for more than two months. And I think that both yourself and Dr. Verrill, while not doubting my measurements, have thought my account of the thickness of the muscular, or rather tendonous husk pretty large, so I am glad to send you the specimens and I will express them packed in salt in a day or two.[9]

Dr. Verrill could not wait. With the specimens in transit, he wrote two new articles on the huge octopus. One, published in February's *American Journal of Science,* formally named the new species *Octopus giganteus,* declaring: "It is possible that it may be related to *Cirroteuthis,* and in that case the two posterior stumps, looking like arms, may be the remains of the lateral fins, for they seem too far back for the arms, unless pulled out of position. On the other hand, they seem to be too far forward for fins. So that they are probably arms twisted out of their true position."[10]

At the same time, Verrill sent another piece to the *New York Herald.* Appearing on 14 February 1897, it read, in part:

> The living weight of the creature was about eighteen or twenty tons. When living, it must have had enormous arms, each one a hundred feet of more in length, each as thick as the mast of a vessel, and armed with hundreds of saucer-shaped suckers, the largest of which would have been at least a foot in diameter....Its eyes would have been more than a foot in diameter. It would have carried ten or twelve gallons of ink in the ink bag. It could swim rapidly, without doubt, but its usual habit would be to crawl slowly over the bottom in deep water in pursuit of prey....We must reflect that wherever this creature had its home, there must be living hundreds or even thousands of others of its kind, probably of equal size, otherwise its race could not be kept up....[11]

With those opinions on record, Verrill prepared to examine the samples of tissue delivered by Webb—and they changed everything.

"Certainly Not a Cephalopod"

Verrill received the relics on 23 February 1897, and on 5 March wrote his third article on the St. Augustine globster, for the April issue of *American Naturalist.* "The supposition that it was an *Octopus,*" he wrote,

> "...was partly based upon its baglike form and partly upon the statements made to me that the stumps of large arms were attached to it at first. This last statement was certainly untrue." Without a shred of proof, Verrill essentially branded John Wilson a liar, calling his description of truncated arms "erroneous and entirely misleading."

The bulk of the carcass, Verrill proposed, could be part of a whale, though

> "what part of any cetacean it might be is still an unsolved puzzle."[12]

In fact, a letter from Dr. Webb to the Smithsonian's Professor Dall, dated 17 March 1897, suggests that Dall influenced Verrill's change of heart. While no comments from Dall have been preserved, pro or con, Webb's letter read:

> "As you already know, Prof. Verrill now says our strange creature cannot be a cephalopod and that he cannot say to what animal it belongs. I do not see how it can be any part of a cetacean as Prof. V. says you suggest. It is simply a great big bag and I do not see how it could be any part of a whale. Now that I have had it brought 6 miles up the beach it is out of the way of the tide and the drifting sand and will have a chance to cure or dry up somewhat. If it were not for the soft mass of the viscera which was so difficult to remove that we left it there would be but little odor. As it is there is no great amount". [13]

On 13 March, *The Tatler* weighed in to say:

> "Professor Verrill of Yale University, who recently decided that the curious something, supposed to be an octopus, was one, basing his decision on the descriptions sent, has now concluded, after examining a piece of it, that it could not possibly be an octopus, and he cannot decide what it is. One theory advanced is that it may be a portion of some inhabitant of the sea, long since extinct, that has been fast in an iceberg for centuries, and recently washed ashore here. Another theory is that it is a portion of a deep-sea monster that on coming too

near the surface was attacked by a shark, who found it too tough for a breakfast. One thing is not determined, and that is, if we do not know what it is, we know what it is not."[14]

Presumably embarrassed, Dr. Verrill sat down on 19 March to write yet another article, this one for the April issue of the *American Journal of Science.* Its title—"The supposed great Octopus of Florida; certainly not a Cephalopod"—was emphatic, and Verrill sought to mask his former indecision by naming the Florida globster as part of a sperm whale. He wrote:

> "The structure of the integument is more like that of the upper part of the head of a sperm whale than any other known to me, and as the obvious use is the same, it is most probable that the whole mass represents the upper part of the head of such a whale, detached from the skull and jaw. It is evident, however, from the figures, that the shape is decidedly unlike the head of an ordinary sperm whale, for the latter is oblong, truncated and rather narrow in front, like the prow of a vessel with an angle at the upper front end, near which a single blow-hole is situated. No blow-hole has been discovered in the mass cast ashore".[15]

Having thus harpooned his own argument, Verrill urged his readers to "imagine a sperm whale with an abnormally large nose, due to disease or old age," admitting that "it seems hardly probable that another allied whale, with such a big nose, remains to be discovered. Notwithstanding these difficulties, my present opinion, that it came from the head of a creature like a sperm whale in structure, is the only one that seems plausible from the facts now ascertained."[16]

Waffling all the way—and stolidly ignoring Dr. Webb's reference to "viscera" inside the supposed giant whale's nose—Verrill risked becoming a laughingstock. Smithsonian curator Frederic Lucas did his best to help Verrill, perhaps referring to Dr. Dall's samples when he said, "The substance looks like blubber, and smells like blubber, and it is blubber, nothing more nor less." Still, the British journal *Natural Science* could not resist chiding Verrill: "The moral of this is that one should not attempt to describe specimens stranded on the coast of Florida, while sitting in one's study in Connecticut."[17]

Lost and Found
There matters rested for another sixty years. Today, no one recalls what became of the Florida globster, though it apparently served as a popular tourist attraction during early 1897. Six decades later, Dr. Forrest Wood—senior scientist and consultant with the Ocean Sciences Department of the Naval Undersea Research and Development Laboratory in San Diego, California—was completing a study of octopus behavior at Florida's Marineland Research Laboratory (now the Whitney Laboratory for Marine Bioscience), when he discovered an old press clipping about the St. Augustine carcass. Intrigued, Wood launched a personal investigation and discovered, through a colleague at the University of Miami Marine Laboratory, that the Smithsonian Institution still possessed a large jar of tissue labeled *Octopus giganteus Verrill.*[18]

Wood next consulted fellow Marineland researcher and University of Florida professor Joseph Gennaro Jr. Invited to view the Smithsonian's samples, Gennaro flew to Washington and found "a glass container about the size of a milk can. Inside it was a murky mixture of cheesecloth, formalin (and I think some alcohol), and half a dozen large white masses of tough fibrous material, each about as large as a good-sized roast." Gennaro's efforts to excise a sample dulled the blades of four dissecting knives in turn, but he finally secured a portion of the globster for examination at his lab in Florida.[19]

Gennaro, a cell biologist, compared the St. Augustine tissue to known samples of whale, squid, and octopus flesh. The results, as described in the March 1971 issue of *Natural History,* were astounding.

> "To my great dismay, no cellular material at all was discernible. Perhaps because the tissue mass had lain for so many days on the beach of St. Augustine, or perhaps because the formaldehyde or alcohol had had insufficient time to penetrate for adequate preservation, nothing of the original cellular architecture remained. I found, however, that my control samples, which had been properly prepared for histological analysis, also failed to show much cellular arrangement. But even more striking than the absence of cellular structure was the presence of distinctive patterns of connective tissue. Differences between contemporary octopus and squid tissue struck the eye immediately, and each was obviously different from the typical pattern of mammalian tissue.
>
> It occurred to me that I might learn something by observing and comparing the connective tissue patterns of the specimens under polarized light. The highly ordered fiber protein molecules oriented in the plane of the section doubly refracted the light and showed up brightly, while those that were perpendicular appeared black.
>
> Now differences between the contemporary squid and octopus samples became very clear. In the octopus, broad bands of fibers passed across the plane of the tissue and were separated by equally broad bands arranged in a perpendicular direction. In the squid there were narrower but also relatively broad bundles arranged in the plane of the section, separated by thin partitions of perpendicular fibers.
>
> It seemed I had found a means to identify the mystery sample after all. I could distinguish between octopus and squid, and

between them and mammals, which display a lacy network of connective tissue fibers.

After 75 years, the moment of truth was at hand. Viewing section after section of the St. Augustine samples, we decided at once, and beyond any doubt, that the sample was not whale blubber. Further, the connective tissue pattern was that of broad bands in the plane of the section with equally broad bands arranged perpendicularly, a structure similar to, if not identical with, that in my octopus sample.

The evidence appears unmistakable that the St. Augustine sea monster was in fact an octopus, but the implications are fantastic. Even though the sea presents us from time to time with strange and astonishing phenomena, the idea of a gigantic octopus, with arms 75 to 100 feet in length and about 18 inches in diameter at the base—a total spread of some 200 feet—is difficult to comprehend".[20]

Indeed. But Gennaro's verdict was not the last word on St. Augustine's globster.

Round Three

By 1985, Gennaro had transferred to New York University's Department of Biology, but he retained his interest in *Octopus giganteus*. That year, he subjected part of the remaining samples to comparative analyses of various amino acids, with control samples including mammalian collagen, tendon, and bone. Following completion of the tests, Gennaro submitted the results to Dr. Roy Mackal, a biochemist at the University of Chicago and a founding member—with Forrest Wood, Bernard Heuvelmans and others—of the International Society of Cryptozoology (ISC). Mackal, in turn, performed further analyses, employing control samples of tissue from *Architeuthis* and other squids, two species of octopus, a spotted dolphin, and a beluga whale. Mackal published their findings in the 1986 issue of the ISC's peer-reviewed journal *Cryptozoology*.[21]

Mackal wrote that "The *O. giganteus* tissue is almost pure collagen, which is precisely what one might expect for an aquatic invertebrate, such as a giant octopus, with a mass of 6,000 kg [13,200 pounds] or more." Therefore, he concluded: "On the basis of Gennaro's histological studies and the present amino acid and Cu [copper] and Fe [iron] analyses, I conclude that, to the extent the preserved *O. giganteus* tissue is representative of the carcass washed ashore at St. Augustine, Florida, in November 1896, it was essentially a huge mass of collagenous protein. Certainly, the tissue was not blubber. I interpret these results as consistent with, and supportive of, Webb and Verrill's identification of the carcass as that of a gigantic cephalopod, probably an octopus, not referable to any known species."[22]

Another vote, then, for the giant octopus—but, once again, it would not be the final word.

Very Like a Whale

Most of DeWitt Webb's original globster photos were thought to be lost at the turn of the twentieth century, though copies of three from January 1897 survived at the Smithsonian Institution and were published for the first time by Roy Mackal, in 1980. The rest resurfaced in 1993, found by California resident Marjorie Blakoner in an album once owned by St. Augustine photographer Van Lockwood.[23] After studying the photos, author Richard Ellis wrote:

> "Despite all the evidence, past and present, most investigators still insist that the St. Augustine monster was a whale. One has only to read the descriptive material and look at the pictures to realize that this is a misidentification. Indeed, if one examined the pictures with no information about the size of the object, there would be no question regarding the animal: It was an octopus".[24]

Photos meant nothing, however, to the next team of analysts, including Gerald Smith Jr. from Indiana University's School of Medicine and three members of the University of Maryland's Department of Zoology: Sidney Pierce, Timothy Maugel, and Eugenie Clark (another ISC board member). This time around, the researchers compared tissue from *O. giganteus* to tissue from an unidentified "blob" beached at Bermuda in 1988, flesh from an octopus mantle, tissue from a humpback whale, plus tendon and skin from a rat's tail. The samples were compared using both amino acid analysis and electron microscopy.[25]

The authors published their results in April 1995, and while they chose to lead with the 1897 "blubber" quote from Frederic Lucas, their findings were not so simple. First, they determined that both the Florida and Bermuda samples consisted of "almost pure collagen....Neither carcass is from a giant octopus nor any other invertebrate, but they are also not from the same species." In fact, they declared, the Florida globster was a homeothermic (warm-blooded) creature, while Bermuda's globster was a poikilothermic (cold-blooded) vertebrate—i.e., some kind of fish. What "enormous warm-blooded vertebrate" washed ashore at St. Augustine? They conclude that it must have been "the remains of a whale, likely the entire skin." Rather smugly, the authors closed with an expression of "profound sadness at ruining a favorite legend."[26]

But had they done any such thing?

I join author Richard Ellis in asking how a whale might lose its "entire skin" in one bag-like mass, washed ashore without a trace of flesh, muscle, or skeletal remains. (The latest study, once again, ignored DeWitt Webb's reference to viscera observed in 1897.) Whalers—now, as in the nineteenth century—remove the flesh and blubber from their kills in strips. As with Professor Verrill's mythical big-nosed sperm whale, there is no case on record of any cetacean, dead or living, popping out of its skin like a molting insect. Ellis is clearly right in his assessment of the 1995 report: "we must conclude that the mysteries remain unsolved and the legend endures."[27]

Last Call—For Now

Authors Pierce, Smith and Maugel returned to the subject of "globsters" in June 2004, accompanied by colleagues Steven Massey and Nicholas Curtis from the University of South Florida, and Carlos

Olavarría from the Centro de Estudios del Cuaternario Fuego-Patagonia y Antártica Punta Arenas, Chile. This time, they were concerned primarily with a carcass stranded on the Chilean coast in July 2003, but their remarks extend to the St. Augustine specimen, the aforementioned Bermuda blob, a second Bermuda carcass, a Tasmanian carcass beached in 1960, and a globster from Nantucket, Massachusetts.[28]

 In their latest study, the team combined DNA analysis with electron microscopy, and despite repeated citations of their 1995 report—which deemed the 1988 Bermuda blob the carcass of some unknown cold-blooded fish—they reached a radically different result. In fact, they declared: "It is clear now that all of these blobs of popular and cryptozoological interest are, in fact, the decomposed remains of large cetaceans....The results, taken together, leave no doubt that all of the blobs examined here—St. Augustine, Bermuda 1, Bermuda 2, Tasmanian West Coast, Nantucket, and Chilean—represent the decomposed remains of great whales of varying species. Once again, to our disappointment, we have not found any evidence that any of the blobs are the remains of gigantic octopods, or sea monsters of unknown species."[29]

 The authors offer no explanation for their apparent error in 1995, concerning the Bermuda remains—and, in fact, misrepresent those findings when they write: "Other relics such as the St. Augustine (Florida) Sea Monster and the Bermuda Blob are still described by some as the remains of a gigantic octopus (*Octopus giganteus*), even though A. E. Verrill—who named the St. Augustine specimen sight unseen—recanted his identification in favor of whale remains, and in spite of microscopic and biochemical analyses showing that they were nothing more than the collagenous matrix of whale blubber (Pierce *et al.,* 1995)."[30] As we have seen, their 1995 report said nothing of the kind concerning the Bermuda globster. The 2004 report is further compromised by citing an erroneous date for the second Bermuda blob's arrival, claiming that it beached in 1997, rather than 1995. That careless error, although minor in itself, spawned a rash of false reports that *three* globsters had washed ashore on Bermuda, in 1988, 1995, and 1997.[31]

Still, those garbled findings satisfied the *New York Times,* which declared on 27 July 2004 that "[t] his does in fact appear to be the end of the great blob story, a tale that began in late 1896 near St. Augustine, Fla., when two boys found a gigantic lump of white, rubbery flesh, 21 feet long, 7 feet wide and weighing perhaps 7 tons."[32] But if the *Times* was satisfied, ignoring contradictions in the two reports published ten years apart, true skeptics recognize that questions still remain unanswered.

References

1.   Bernard Heuvelmans, *The Kraken and the Colossal Octopus* (London: Routledge, 2003), p. 273; Roy Mackal, *Searching for Hidden Animals: An Inquiry into Zoological Mysteries* (New York: Doubleday, 1980), pp. 36-7.
2.   Heuvelmans, *Kraken,* p. 274-5; Mackal, p. 38.
3.   Richard Ellis, *Monsters of the Sea* (New York: Knopf, 1994), pp. 303-4.
4.   Ibid., p. 304.
5.   Addison Verrill, "A gigantic Cephalopod on the Florida coast," *American Journal of Science* ser. 4, 3 (January 1897): 79.
6.   Heuvelmans, *Kraken,* p. 274.

7. Ellis, p. 306.
8. Ibid.
9. Ibid.
10. Addison Verrill, "Additional information concerning the giant Cephalopod of Florida," *American Journal of Science* ser. 4, 3 (February 1897): 162-163.
11. Ellis, p. 307.
12. Mackal, p. 42; Addison Verrill, "The Florida Sea-Monster," *American Naturalist* 31 (April 1897): 304-7.
13. Ellis, p. 308.
14. Ibid., pp. 308-9.
15. Addison Verrill, "The supposed great Octopus of Florida; certainly not a Cephalopod," *American Journal of Science* ser. 4, 3 (April 1897): 355-356.
16. Ibid.
17. Ellis, p. 310; Heuvelmans, *Kraken,* pp. 275-6.
18. "St. Augustine Monster," Wikipedia, http://en.wikipedia.org/wiki/St._Augustine_Monster; Mackal, pp. 34-5.
19. Mackal, pp. 35-6, 42-3.
20. Forrest Wood and Joseph Gennaro Jr., "An Octopus Trilogy," *Natural History* 80 (March 1971): 15-24, 84-7.
21. Roy Mackal, "Biochemical Analyses of Preserved *Octopus giganteus* Tissue," *Cryptozoology* 5: 56-60.
22. Ibid., pp. 60-1.
23. Mackal, *Searching,* pp. 39-41; "St. Augustine Monster," Wikipedia.
24. Ellis, pp. 319-20.
25. Sidney Pierce, Gerald Smith Jr., Timothy Maugel and Eugene Clark, "On the Giant Octopus (*Octopus giganteus*) and the Bermuda Blob: Homage to A. E. Verrill," *Biological Bulletin* 188 (April 1995): 220-25.
26. Ibid., pp. 228-9.
27. Ellis, p. 322.
28. Sidney Pierce, Steven Massey, Nicholas Curtis, Gerald Smith Jr., Carlos Olavarria and Timothy Maugel, "Microscopic, Biochemical, and Molecular Characteristics of the Chilean Blob and a Comparison With the Remains of Other Sea Monsters: Nothing but Whales," *Biological Bulletin* 2006 (June 2004): 125-33.
29. Ibid.
30. Ibid.
31. Michael Newton, "A 'Blob' That Never Was," Still on the Track, 20 March 2011, http://forteanzoology.blogspot.com/2011/03/michael-newton-blob-that-never-was.html.
32. William Broad, "Ogre? Octopus? Blobologists Solve an Ancient Mystery," *New York Times*, 27 July 2004.

2.

Champlain Bubbles

Chasing Champ

Dividing New York from Vermont, with its northern tip in Canada, Lake Champlain is 110 miles long, with a surface area of 435 square miles. Its average depth is sixty-four feet, with a maximum recorded depth of 440 feet. It bears the name of French explorer Samuel de Champlain, who "discovered" it in 1609, with help from aboriginal scouts. Some accounts claim that Champlain was also the first European to sight the lake's legendary cryptid—later dubbed "Champ"—but those reports stem from an erroneous "quotation" from Champlain's diary, published by the *Vermont Journal* in 1970.[1]

In fact, the first "genuine" Champ sighting dates from July 1819, with 339 recorded by July 2005. American showman Phineas Taylor Barnum offered $50,000 for Champ's capture in 1873, scaled back to $20,000 in 1887, but neither bid produced a specimen.[2]

Most lake monster believers agree that the best evidence of Champ's existence is a photograph snapped on 5 July 1977 and published for the first time four years later.

Anthony and Sandra Mansi (then engaged to be married), with two children from Sandra's previous marriage, had camped at Vergennes, Vermont, on 4 July, and stopped along the lake's shore the following day, near St. Albans. While the children played, Sandra noted a disturbance in the water, some 150 feet offshore. At first, she took it for "an elephant tuna fish," then a scuba diver, until a "dinosaur" head and neck rose some six feet above the surface.[3] As she described what happened next:

The rest of the neck came out of the water and then the hump came out. And it looked around, it never swam, it just looked around, like this. And it was the texture like that of an eel. You know how an eel looks slimy and shiny if the light is on it somewhat. That was the texture of it. It was kind of slow moving and really quite majestic. But I was terrified. And I thought that sucker had legs and was coming out on shore.[4]

Before fleeing with her family, Sandra snapped a photo with her Kodak Instamatic camera, placing it in an album and keeping the incident secret until autumn 1979, when she contacted Dr. Philip Reines, professor of communications at State University of New York in Plattsburgh. Reines introduced Mansi to Champ researcher Joseph Zarzynski, who in turn delivered the photo to Dr. George Zug, then curator of reptiles and amphibians at the Smithsonian National Museum of Natural History in Washington, D.C.

On 9 July 1980, Dr. Zug wrote to Zarzynski: "The Mansi photograph is fascinating and quite good considering the circumstances under which it was taken. Unfortunately, I can offer no equivocal identification....Certainly all our examinations cast no doubts on the authenticity of their photograph and report."[5]

Zarzynski next contacted Dr. Roy Mackal at the University of Chicago, who sent Mansi's photo to colleague J. Richard Greenwell, British-born coordinator for the Office of Arid Land Studies at the University of Arizona and a founder of the ISC. Greenwell arranged for Dr. B. Roy Frieden, a mathematical physicist, to examine the photo at UA's Optical Sciences Center. Frieden's report, issued on 30 April 1981, declared that "the photo does not appear to be a montage or a superimposition of any kind." The sole "suspicious detail" was a horizontal "brownish streak," identified as a probable sandbar by some unnamed former resident of Lake Champlain's vicinity whom Frieden consulted. While accepting that judgment without further evidence, Frieden granted that "There is another school of thought that says since it's dark, maybe it means deep water."[6]

If it was a sandbar, Frieden wrote, "there is a distinct possibility that the object was put there by someone, either the people who took the photo or by the people who were fooling them, because you could simply walk out on such a sand bar and tow the object behind you and hide behind it as you made it rise out of the water and so forth....[I]f the sand bar question is resolved and the fact that it's not a sand bar can be really confirmed, then there's much smaller likelihood of this being a hoax."[7]

Three decades after the fact, the sandbar question has not been resolved (though some skofftics take it for granted), yet questions remain. It seems impossible that any third party could drag a makeshift monster out from shore in full view of the Mansis, then submerge it (on a sandbar!) and make it rise again, all while remaining invisible. Thus, if there was a willful hoax, logic dictates that the Mansis must have been active participants.

There is no rational alternative.
The *New York Times* broke Mansi's story on 30 June 1981, with a summary of Dr. Frieden's findings and a black-and-white print of the photo. By then, the *Times* announced, the photo's negative was missing. *Maclean's* and *Time* magazines ran copies of the original color photo simultaneously on 13 July 1981. Predictably, the ensuing debate was intense.

Next to weigh in on the Mansi photo was Dr. Paul LeBlond, head of the Department of Earth and Ocean Sciences at the University of British Columbia and a founding director of the ISC. Writing for the premiere issue of the society's peer-reviewed journal in winter 1982, Dr.

LeBlond offered an estimate of Champ's dimensions calculated from surrounding waves. Using the Beaufort scale to estimate wind speed from the appearance of the lake's surface, LeBlond gauged the distance between visible waves, thus determining that "Champ stretches from 1.5 to 2 wavelengths at the water line: this dimension ranges from an extreme lower bound of 4.8m [16 feet] to an extreme upper bound of 17.2m [56 feet]." Thus, the original Mansi estimates of Champ's total length as twelve to fifteen feet (Sandra) or fifteen to twenty feet (Anthony) fell within the lower possible size range. Dr. LeBlond also dismissed the hidden sandbar hypothesis as "inconsistent with the behavior of the waves traveling over that area."[8]

While Dr. LeBlond was preparing his piece for *Cryptozoology*, the ISC's newsletter broke further news from Arizona, where Roy Frieden had subjected the Mansi photo to electronic enhancement and reverse image contrast processing. Based on those studies, he concluded that the photo "did demonstrate that the monster's 'back' and 'head' are connected (not clearly visible to the eye in the original print)." However, the enhancement "could not resolve the facial features because the head was heavily shadowed."[9]

S.I. Investigates

Enter the staff of *Skeptical Inquirer*, published since 1976 by a group pledged to "promote scientific inquiry, critical investigation, and the use of reason in examining controversial and extraordinary claims," presently known as the Committee for Skeptical Inquiry. Two "research fellows" of the CSI—*S.I.* columnist Joe Nickell and managing editor Benjamin Radford—spent a total of eight days at Lake Champlain in August 2002, during which they reportedly "examined all aspects of the Champ legend, from its alleged inception, through the impact of a famous 1977 photograph of the creature, and beyond," modestly declaring their effort "the most wide-ranging, hands-on investigation of Champ ever conducted with an intent to solve, rather than promote, the mystery."[10]

On 22 August alone, according to Nickell, they interviewed a New York skeptic and his cryptozoologist brother, then "began to explore Lake Champlain from its southernmost tip near Whitehall to its northern end in Québec." Subsequent days included lakeside vigils, observation of a sign listing Champ sightings, and a visit to a local bar, where one self-proclaimed witness declared all others to be drunkards. By the time the intrepid explorers departed, their disbelief in Champ was (not surprisingly) confirmed and carved in stone.[11]

Even so, another year passed before Nickell and Radford published their findings, in two parts, for *S.I.*'s July/August issue of 2003. Nickell dealt with Champ's "legend," citing inconsistencies in media reports and eyewitness descriptions, describing the phenomenon of "expectant attention" that prompts sightings of monsters where none exist, and blaming the "bandwagon effect" for proliferation of sightings in specific years. The net result: "Not only is there not a single piece of convincing evidence for Champ's existence, but there are many reasons against it, one of which is that a single monster can neither live for centuries nor reproduce itself."[12]

A claim, we should note, that has never been advanced by any serious researcher. As alert as he is to misuse of propaganda techniques by others, Nickell nonetheless seems willing to use the duplicitous "straw man" approach, dismantling arguments employed by no one other than himself.

Radford was left to debunk the Mansi photo. He began by interviewing Sandra herself on 24 August 2002, but directly quotes only fifty-seven words from her statement in a 3,433-word article. Despite selective editing, Mansi did not appear to contradict her original statements from 1981, which left Radford to raise "The Hoaxing Question."[13]

First, he noted that "the photo has virtually no objects of known scale (boat, human, etc.) by which to judge the creature's size or the distance," a fact which—while accurate—assumes significance only if the photo was hoaxed.[14] By definition, photographs of unexpected incidents cannot be staged for the subsequent convenience of armchair analysts, by including mundane objects missing from the scene as events unfold.

Next, Radford declared, "The fact that the Mansis, allegedly afraid of ridicule, waited four years to release the photo was also seen [by Radford] as suspicious. All we are left with is a fantastic story whose only supporting proof is a compelling but ambiguous photograph of something in the water."[15] The same result would exist, of course, if the Mansis had broadcast their story and photo in July 1977. The hypocrisy of this argument only becomes apparent when—as revealed in subsequent chapters—we find skeptics eager to accept wholly unsubstantiated "hoax confessions" aired for the first time forty to sixty years after the fact.

Following that lead-in, Radford left the Mansis to attack Dr. Richard D. Smith, head of New Jersey-based Wind & Whalebone Media Productions, who wrote of Mansi's photo in 1983: "As a photographer and filmmaker, I can speak with some authority as to what it would take to fake a picture of this sort. Assuming the remote possibility that the Mansi photo is a fraud, it would require fabrication of an excellent, full-sized model (highly expensive in terms of expertise and materials) which would have to be smuggled out to Champlain or another lake, there assembled or inflated, and successfully maneuvered around out in the water (most difficult, especially with a slight wind blowing), the whole thing accomplished without being seen or the slightest leak in security (unlikely)."[16]

Radford—who wrote, directed and produced two short animated films years after penning his 2003 article on Champ, thus making him a retroactive "expert" on all aspects the medium[17]—deems Smith's opinion "nearly comical in its strained assumptions," particularly with regard to a life-sized model of Champ being used by the Mansis, or by someone attempting to dupe them. What explanation, then, remains? Radford magnanimously declares himself "willing to grant that [Mansi] is probably a sincere eyewitness reporting essentially what she saw."[18]

But *what* did she see?

Radford's first suggestion is the sandbar suggested by Dr. Frieden in 1981 and confidently dismissed by Dr. LeBlond a year later. Unable to resolve that contradiction, he states categorically (but without proof, beyond his personal assertion) that LeBlond was "clearly wrong" in plotting the probable location of Mansi's sighting on a map of Lake Champlain. That said, he drops the sandbar argument and veers off in a new direction for "The Radford Analysis."[19]

Ignoring the report from Dr. Frieden, quoted in the *ISC Newsletter* twenty-one years earlier, Radford notes "an odd thing" about Mansi's photo. Specifically, "It is not apparent at first glance, but the 'head' and 'hump' are not clearly connected." Without the benefit of Dr. Frieden's wisdom and equipment, Radford speculates that Mansi's creature may be two separate objects coincidentally juxtaposed, the apparent head and neck "perhaps a gnarled tree root branching away at an angle."[20]

After conducting various experiments to prove his point—allegedly measuring Champ in Mansi's original photo, wading out from shore with a "mock Champ," etc.—Radford concluded that "for those claiming that the Mansi object is huge, the numbers don't add up." In his view, the presumed neck is barely three feet high, while the whole object stretches seven feet from end to end. Again, no computations are provided to contest Dr. LeBlond's work from the Beaufort scale. The net result: "If the main eyewitness is to be believed [*sic*], this 'extremely good evidence' for Champ (and, by extension, other lake monsters) is even weaker than previously suspected."[21]

On Second Thought ...
Radford tried for another bite at the apple nine months later, with a new article and hypothesis in the April 2004 issue of *Fortean Times*. Moving steadily away from his prior assessment of Sandra Mansi as "a sincere eyewitness reporting essentially what she saw," Radford laments that "remarkably little progress has been made in identifying [the photo's] subject" since his last attempt. Now, he implies conspiracy.[22]

"Whether by accident or design, " Radford writes, "virtually all of the information needed to determine the photograph's authenticity is missing, lost or unavailable. For example, Mansi cannot provide the negative, which might show evidence of tampering, neither can she provide other photographs from the roll (which might show other angles of the same object, or perhaps 'test' photos of a known object from an odd position). Mansi is unable to locate the site of the photo, which would help to determine a number of things, including the size of the object, and the photo itself shows virtually no objects of known scale by which to judge the creature's size or distance."[23]

Tackling "the most fundamental question"—whether Champ is alive or a posed, inanimate object—Radford judged the angle of head and neck "very unnatural," declaring that "[i]t is hard to conceive of a large, aquatic animal whose morphology would allow for such a tortuous positioning." Mansi's 1981 description of a creature seemingly insensible to noise and movement on the shore further convinced Radford that "the object could not hear because it was inanimate." Setting up his pitch, he told his readers: "Finally, we have Sandra Mansi's description of the object's texture. In her words, the object was wet and glistening and its texture was 'like bark, like crevice-ey...' Perhaps, then, it was bark."[24]

Perhaps ... except that Radford's article cites no source for Mansi's comment—which, as we have seen, flatly contradicts her longstanding description of Champ's skin as having a "texture like that of an eel...slimy and shiny." Radford's previous piece for *Skeptical Inquirer* includes no mention of "crevice-ey" skin, nor does any other retrievable source. If Mansi provided this contradictory description in her 2002 interview with Radford, why not cite it?

Whatever its provenance, the "crevice-ey" quote banished Radford's suspicion of conspiracy, reinstating Sandra Mansi as "an honest person" in his estimation. Concluding that the object in her photo "had none of the characteristics of a living animal," Radford dropped his original two-piece Champ and offered a drifting log as "The Best Candidate." Not just any log, mind you, but one uniquely resembling a plesiosaur. Radford allegedly photographed one such piece of driftwood beached at Lake Champlain, and while it clearly does resemble a monster of some kind (minus any sense of scale, a hoaxer's cardinal sin), it had nothing whatever in common with Mansi's subject. To bridge that yawning gap, Radford resorted to pen and paper, sketching an imaginary "monster" log with all the necessary bits and posing it in sundry attitudes to seal the deal. Even then, he conceded, "I cannot conclusively prove the object is a tree; fortunately, I don't have to."[25]

No, indeed. Those who question his solution are required (by Radford) to prove the nonexistence of a most convenient log that Radford himself never found, at Lake Champlain or anywhere else.

A Model Explanation

In 2006, Radford and Nickell recycled their Champ articles more or less verbatim in a book, *Lake Monster Mysteries*, published by the University Press of Kentucky. Their introduction proclaims the book "unique in several respects," but cites only one, saying: "Many books on this topic are not so much *written* as *compiled*, consisting essentially of collections of entertaining stories and legends written to entice and amuse. Little if any attempt is made to actually investigate the sightings or even treat the subject as a mystery to be solved." [Emphasis in the original.] And again, "Rather than simply cataloging the sightings, we have chosen a different path: in-depth, hands-on investigations."[26]

That said, readers may be surprised to find that, while Radford and Nickell treat twenty alleged "monster " lakes in varying detail, they only describe personal visits to five, with no substantive details provided for three of those "expeditions." Indeed, by actual page-count, treatment of Champ accounts for 30 percent of their text overall. Information on most of the others is simply compiled from pre-existing sources, with no apparent "hands-on" work in evidence.[27]

As for entertainment, it is difficult to top the authors' claim that "such investigations might be dangerous," prompting them to review their insurance policies "for the 'psychological aftershocks' we might endure if we were fortunate enough to come face-to-face with one of these creatures." The "threat" from nonexistent monsters, including two notorious hoaxes thoroughly debunked in 1855 and 1904 respectively, goes unexplained.[28]

Nickell's portion of the book's Champ chapter is simply his 2003 *S.I.* article, treated to a cosmetic makeover. Selective phrases are revised—"friend and fellow skeptic Robert Bartholomew" becomes "friend and fellow researcher Robert Bartholomew," etc.—but *S.I.* subscribers may feel that they've wasted $26.95 on a retread.[29] Radford is more imaginative, borrowing text from his *Fortean Times* article in addition to the older *S.I.* piece, repeating Mansi's alleged description of bark-like skin (now spelled "crevice-y"), still without a citation.[30]

In addition to reprinting photos from his other articles, Radford trumps his *FT* drawings with photos of an identical monster log sculpted from clay, in miniature. Dubbing it an "animated sequence," he presents four snapshots of the imaginary log in poses meant to mimic Mansi's Champ, perched atop a transparent blade of some kind to hold the model in midair. Curiously, two of the four resultant photos bear no resemblance to Mansi's subject, and actual animation of the sequence would present a figure flopping and rolling in a manner totally unlike Mansi's description of Champ as she saw it.[31]

Despite repeated descriptions of Sandra Mansi as "an honest person" and "a sincere eyewitness," Radford still regards her as both mistaken and brainwashed by overzealous cryptozoologists. To prove the latter point, Radford declares his still-unpublished 2002 interview with Mansi "the basis of comparison" for all other statements she's made, either before or since that date. According to Radford, the Mansis initially thought that the object they'd seen was "probably a fish." They "totally dismissed" any notion of Champ until the photo was developed, whereupon they "considered the possibility" but remained apathetic. Only after three years of exposure to pesky researchers was Mansi converted into a Champ believer. Thus, Radford explains, "cryptozoologists created a monster."[32]

In fact, if we believe Radford and Nickell, Sandra Mansi is not the only victim of extreme suggestibility where lake monsters are concerned. They see a parallel in the case of "Memphré," a supposed cryptid reported since 1816 from Lake Memphrémagog, on the Vermont-Québec border. Radford and Nickell devote a scant four pages of text to Memphré in their book on lake monsters, with no evidence of the "in-depth, hands-on investigation" promised to their readers. Half of the miniscule chapter, in fact, is devoted to controversial witness Barbara Malloy, whose first sighting of Memphré dates from August 1983. Radford and Nickell find it terribly significant that Malloy—"like Mansi, a middle-aged Vermont woman"—logged her sighting "just two years" after Mansi's photo was published. Without explaining their double-barreled cheap shot at Vermonters and middle-aged females, the authors proclaim: "Lake monster sightings almost invariably correspond with the public's interest in the creatures, suggesting a social and cultural engine...behind the reports."[33] In which case, one might ask: Why wait two years?

In closing, Radford assures us that he does not "flatly discount the idea of large, unknown creatures in Lake Champlain," but that claim—like his protestations of Sandra Mansi's sincerity—ring hollow as he beats the drum for a potential hoax. Disclaimers of a fraud, he says, are "comical," "strained," and "far-fetched." The indicators of a hoax, in Radford's view, are numerous: a single, high-quality photo taken by chance; Mansi's loss of the negative; her inability to pinpoint the encounter site; and the four-year delay in publication. All, he tells us, suggestive of the very hoax of which Radford himself exonerates Sandra Mansi.[34]

Let us be clear: if the Mansi photo is a hoax, Sandra herself must be responsible. With that in mind, and assuming a fraud, what might be its motive?

Profit springs to mind ... but whose? A genuine lake monster photo might be worth millions, yet Ben Radford concedes that Mansi has rejected various lucrative offers for rights to her photo.[35] Most published versions of the photo include a caption naming Mansi and the Gamma Liaison Photo Agency as joint copyright holders for the Champ snapshot, but my inquiries to Gamma Liaison in 2004 produced a response that the agency no longer handles the Mansi photo. In response to that observation, posted online in 2010, Radford wrote: "It's reprinted in my 2007 book [*sic*], and I know exactly who to contact for permission to use the image, and even the current rate ($1,000)." His version of the photograph—published in 2006, not 2007—credits Mansi alone as the copyright holder.[36]

In parting—blissfully ignorant of my own repeated visits to Loch Ness spanning a quarter-century—Radford felt compelled to add: "It's a shame Newton is so quick to dismiss and criticize others who are actually out there doing research, investigations, and experiments. I'm out there taking the subject seriously, doing real work and real investigation and trying to contribute while Newton sits in his armchair and takes potshots."[37] This, ironically, from a man who declares himself both the enemy and victim of personal insults—described, by him, as "a version of the logical fallacy of the ad hominem attack: Criticizing the person, not the argument or claim. We see it all the time in skepticism; it's nothing new. But when a colleague and ostensible critical thinker does it, it's disheartening."[38]

What else remains, as motive for a hoax, once profit is removed? Reality TV has taught us that some people will do anything to claim a tawdry moment in the spotlight, but Sandra Mansi's personal behavior does not seem to fit that mold. Nothing reveals her as an inveterate practical joker. There is no hint of malice in her actions—and even if there was, its target would remain obscure.

Floating log or monster? Hoax, sincere mistake, or accurate report of an encounter with a real-life cryptid? At thirty-six years and counting, we shall likely never know. But if skeptics are correct in saying that the Mansi photo fails to prove Champ's case, so sketches and models of hypothetical logs fall far short of proving the creature a myth. The contest is a draw.

The mystery remains.

References

1. "Champ, the Lake Champlain 'Monster,'" Paranormal Encyclopedia, http://www.paranormal-encyclopedia.com/c/champ.
2. Gary Mangiacopra and Dwight Smith, *Does Champ Exist?* (Landisville, PA: Coachwhip Publications, 2007), pp. 172-210; Joseph Zarzynski, *Champ: Beyond the Legend* (Chesterfield, Derbyshire: Bannister Publications, 1984), p. 83.
3. Zarzynski, pp. 62-3.
4. Mangiacopra and Smith, p. 58.
5. Zarzynski, p. 63.
6. Ibid., pp. 140-1.
7. Ibid., pp. 141-2.
8. Paul LeBlond, "An Estimate of the Dimensions of the Lake Champlain Monster from the Length of Adjacent Wind Waves in the Mansi Photograph," *Cryptozoology* 1 (Winter 1982): 54-60.
9. Anonymous, "Lake Champlain monster draws worldwide attention," *ISC Newsletter* 1 (Summer 1982): 1-4.
10. Joe Nickell, "Legend of the Lake Champlain Monster," *Skeptical Inquirer* 27 (July/August 2003), http://www.csicop.org/si/show/legend_of_the_lake_champlain_monster.
11. Ibid.
12. Ibid.
13. Ben Radford, "The Measure of a Monster: Investigating the Champ Photo," *Skeptical Inquirer* 27 (July/August 2003), http://www.csicop.org/si/show/measure_of_a_monster_investigating_the_champ_photo.
14. Ibid.
15. Ibid.
16. Zarzynski, p. 69.
17. "Benjamin Radford," Wikipedia, http://en.wikipedia.org/wiki/Benjamin_Radford; "Benjamin Radford," IMDB, http://www.imdb.com/name/nm2727023.
18. Radford, "The Measure of a Monster."
19. Ibid.
20. Ibid.
21. Ibid.
22. Benjamin Radford, "Lake Champlain Monster," *Fortean Times* (April 2004), http://www.forteantimes.com/features/articles/157/lake_champlain_monster.html.
23. Ibid.
24. Ibid.
25. Ibid.
26. Benjamin Radford and Joe Nickell, *Lake Monster Mysteries* (Lexington, KY: University Press of Kentucky, 2006), pp. 7-8.
27. Ibid., pp. 11-147.
28. Ibid., pp. 9, 79-88, 101-9.
29. Ibid., pp. 28-43; Joe Nickell, "Legend of the Lake Champlain Monster."
30. Radford and Nickell, pp. 43-59; Radford, "The Measure of a Monster"; Radford, "Lake Champlain Monster."

31. Radford and Nickell, pp. 165-7.
32. Ibid., 153-5, 157.
33. Ibid., pp. 7, 71-6, 156.
34. Ibid., pp. 45-7.
35. Ibid., p. 46.
36. Ben Radford posting to *Still on the Track*, Centre for Fortean Zoology, 20 June 2010, http://forteanzoology.blogspot.com/2010/06/michael-newton-champlain-bubbles.html; Radford and Nickell, p. 44.
37. Radford posting to *Still on the Track*, 20 June 2010.
38. Ben Radford, "Haters, Bias, and Skeptical Inquiry," Benjamin Radford, http://benjaminradford.com/2011/10/06/haters-bias-and-skeptical-inquiry.

3.
Muddying Clearwater

Old Three-Toes
In the mid-1930s, large three-toed footprints appeared on lonely beaches ranging from Queensland, Tasmania, and New Zealand to Patagonia and Nantucket, Massachusetts. The year 1937 brought similar reports from Natal, South Africa, where witness Aleko Lilius photographed footprints and claimed to have fired on their hulking, reptilian maker. Strangely, Lilius also claimed that some of the tracks were faked by a Zulu witch doctor, which left the story dangling in uncertainty.[1]

Fast-forward to February 1948, on the west coast of Florida. Early one morning, date unknown, two young lovers told police they had been interrupted by "a monster" rising from the surf at Clearwater. Daylight brought discovery of large three-toed tracks on the beach, with more appearing on 6 March, a mile and a half north of the first site. On 20 March the action shifted southward, to Dan's Island. On 3 April a 350-yard line of footprints appeared at Indian Rocks, 10 miles south of Clearwater. Some time later, date again unknown, more tracks were found at Philip's Hammock, on Tampa Bay.[2]

The next eyewitness sighting of an unknown creature—and the first with witnesses identified—occurred on 25 July. Two instructors from the Dunedin Flying School, John Milner and George Orfanides, were circling over the Gulf of Mexico at 200 feet when they saw a large creature swimming near Hog Island (now Caladesi Island). They judged it to be 15 feet long, with a "very hairy body, a heavy blunt head and back legs like an alligator but much heavier. The tail [was] long and blunt." Rushing back to their airstrip, the witnesses picked up associates Mario Hernandez and Francis Whillock, then flew back to Hog Island. They found the beast again and made a dozen passes to observe it, later stating that it had four legs "pressed under the body most of the time."[3]

In August a pair of tourists from Milwaukee, fishing from a rowboat among the Anclote Keys, north of Tarpon Springs, saw a large gray object ashore. They first mistook it for a tent, then watched it waddle off into the surf, describing it as "having a head like a rhinoceros but with no neck. It sort of flowed into its narrow shoulders. It was gray and covered with short thick fur. It had short, very thick legs and huge feet, and from its shoulders hung two flippers. It didn't run into the water, or dive in; it sort of slid in sidewise."[4]

Two more sightings occurred in October. On the 21st, several members of a local Baptist church were picnicking beside the Suwannee River, near Chiefland, when they saw "a dome-shaped, rough and knobby object" in the water. All assumed it was a log, until they noticed that it swam upstream, against the river's current. On the same day, a new trail of 242 three-toed footprints appeared at Suwannee Gables, near Old Town. Three days later, witness Mary Belle Smith saw "a very large, dun-colored animal" paddling in the Suwannee, near the point where Highway 19 bridged the river.[5]

On the Track
Meanwhile, a thousand miles to the north, Three-Toes was making waves in New York City. Reports from Clearwater raised eyebrows at the *New York Herald-Tribune* and in the boardroom of the National Broadcasting Company. Together, those media giants commissioned an on-site investigation.

Their first and only choice to lead the expedition: Ivan Terrence Sanderson.

A native Scotsman, Sanderson held a B.A. with honors in zoology from England's Cambridge University, buttressed by M.A. degrees in botany and geology. His passion was wildlife, pursued in every corner of the globe, including various bizarre encounters that would fuel a lifelong interest in cryptozoology. Settled in New Jersey after World War II, he soon became a fixture on radio and television, educating Americans to the lifestyles of exotic species. He was, in short, Jack Hanna and Steve Irwin, rolled up into one.

Who better to investigate an unknown critter at large in America's southern playground?

Sanderson first heard of Three-Toes in July 1948, then embarked for Clearwater in mid-October. Only one set of footprints—from 21 October—remained by the time he arrived, but Sanderson examined them minutely. The left foot measured 13.41 inches from its heel to the tip of its clawed middle toe, while the right was 13.5 inches long. As to depth, depending on the soil, prints ranged from three-quarters of an inch to two inches deep.[6]

Sanderson later wrote: "We were told by several people who had observed the tracks when fresh—and these included the local police—that the imprints were originally clearly defined on the hardest sand, although we were unable to make any impression on this by stamping or even by throwing a 35-pound lead model of the imprints down upon it from a height of three feet."[7]

And again: "*When we attempted to reproduce them with 35-pound lead models strapped to the writer's feet, no impression whatsoever was left on the ball-bearing sand when it was wet, and impressions made in medium or soft mud were surrounded by an impact ridge that completely surrounded the imprint. No such ridge at any time appeared around any imprint at Clearwater, on the Suwannee, or elsewhere.*"[8][Italics in the original.]

Highway engineers, consulted by Sanderson, opined that "if made physically by a man, either with devices strapped to his feet or on stilts," the Florida tracks would require "a ton on each leg" as "the absolute minimum weight" to produce the impressions discovered.[9]

Weight aside, Sanderson's initial suspicion of a hoax floundered on the variations seen in individual footprints. Examining the tracks, he found one point where they had climbed an embankment, gouging claw marks three inches deep with no trace of the foot's ball or heel. Elsewhere, he saw that "the middle toe could on occasion be held up by a root while the outer and inner toes not only reached the ground but gouged deep claw incisions into its surface," an impression "manifestly impossible of reproduction with any rigid device." In yet another print, the toes were seen to "spread by as much as 15° and slip under small sticks."[10]

Finally, if any further evidence were needed, Sanderson himself sighted the creature while flying above the Suwannee River with *Herald-Tribune* pilot Lloyd Rondeau, midway between Old Town and the river's mouth. Both men saw an "enormous dirty-yellow colored creature rolling about on the surface of the water, making a huge lozenge-shaped patch of foam on the dark waters all around it," but the beast vanished while they circled back to make another pass. Sanderson later wrote that "the same thing" was seen at Dundein, on 14 November, but no further details are known of the creature's last appearance.[11] Sanderson left Florida two days later, to compile his findings.

The release of Ivan Sanderson's fifty-three-page report sent Three-Toes packing. At home in New Jersey, Sanderson divided his time between straightforward nature writing (with his first book, *How to Know the American Mammals*, published in 1951) and excursions into Forteana. In 1965 he founded the Society for the Investigation of the Unexplained (SITU) and launched its journal, *Pursuit*, pledged to "the acquisition, investigation and dissemination of information on reports of all tangible items in the fields of chemistry, astronomy, geology, biology and anthropology, that are not readily explained."

Sanderson revisited the Three-Toes case two decades after his Florida expedition, in a pair of articles published by *Fate* magazine. The December 1967 issue covered cases from the latter 1930s, while Sanderson recited 1948's events in January 1968, suggesting for the first time that the creature may have been an unknown giant penguin. A year later, both articles appeared as consecutive chapters in *More "Things,"* a collection of Sanderson's magazine pieces published by Pyramid Books.

Stomach cancer claimed Sanderson's life on 19 February 1973. SITU briefly survived him, then disbanded. In Florida, Three-Toes was seemingly forgotten.

A Monster Unmasked?
Fifteen years and four months after Sanderson's death, reporter Jan Kirby wrote an article for the *St. Petersburg Times*, headlined "Clearwater Can Relax; Monster is Unmasked." Opening with a wholly unsubstantiated claim that three-toed tracks "appeared frequently" throughout western Florida for a decade after 1948, Kirby proceeded to say that "a number of local people, including the police, believed the whole thing was a hoax," but "had no way to prove it."[12]

Chief among the doubters, Kirby said, was ex-police chief Frank Daniels, who allegedly blamed the footprints on Al Williams, an inveterate practical joker and owner of Clearwater's Auto Electric shop. Daniels told Kirby, "We suspected Williams because he usually called in the reports of the monster and was such a local prankster....When a pilot flying over the beaches reported seeing something furry with a head shaped like a hog's in the Gulf, we suspected Williams because he flew his own plane."[13]

Kirby proved herself gullible by accepting those claims at face value. First, we know from coverage of events in 1948 that Al Williams did not report "most" of the footprint discoveries or cryptid sightings. In fact, his name appears nowhere on any published list of witnesses. Furthermore, Daniels implies that the pilot who reported a hog-headed creature to police was unidentified, thus "suspected" of being Williams. He was, in fact, John Milner, accompanied by George Orfanides, Mario Hernandez, and Frank Whillock. The only other sighting from an aircraft involved Ivan Sanderson and pilot Lloyd Rondeau. Al Williams played no part in either incident.

Unable to question Williams, deceased since 1969, Kirby turned to his business partner, Tony Signorini, with whom she says Williams "left the secret of the 'Clearwater Monster' for safekeeping." There was more to the story, however, since Signorini claimed he *was* the monster, cavorting on beaches and river banks with a pair of thirty-pound lead "monster" feet attached to high-top tennis shoes.[14]

How did he make the tracks described by Ivan Sanderson as falling beyond human fabrication? According to Signorini, "I would just swing my leg back and forth like this and then give a big hop, and the weight of the feet would carry me [six feet]. The shoes were heavy enough to sink down in the sand."[15]

Indeed? What of Sanderson's experiments, using lead feet five pounds heavier than Signorini's? How does Tony's tale explain the tracks that showed only toe marks climbing embankments? And how on Earth did the rigid middle toes of Tony's lead boots flex and rise while walking over tree roots, or perform the other movements cataloged by Sanderson?

Likewise, while Signorini's hopping gait might explain an occasional six-foot stride, artificial feet twice the size of his own could just as easily *reduce* the space between his footsteps. And, as Sanderson reported in 1948, the tracks typically displayed a stride ranging from twenty-five to thirty-one inches, far less than six feet, thus belying Tony's description of marathon leap-fests by moonlight.

Next, we have Kirby's spurious claim that "the 'monster' came out only at night."[16] Signorini and Williams may have been nocturnal hoaxers, but large unidentified creatures were seen in the flesh by more than a dozen persons during the 1948 monster flap. All but one of those incidents occurred in broad daylight. All but one involved multiple witnesses.

Finally, why did Signorini wait forty years to reveal his practical joke? According to Kirby, he was "encouraged" to tell all by various friends, after Al Williams died in 1969. He thus agreed to "bring the monster out of hiding," yet inexplicably stalled for another nineteen years.[17]

Across the country and around the world, journalists rushed to trumpet Signorini's tale without a hint of critical fact-checking. Curiously, one publication that climbed aboard the bandwagon was a quarterly newsletter published by the International Society of Cryptozoology. While acknowledging—then otherwise ignoring—Ivan Sanderson's technical report from 1948, The *ISC Newsletter* reprinted Jan Kirby's article verbatim and capped it by commending Signorini for his belated revelation, rating his fraud as "one of the best and most colorful hoaxes of all time."[18] The various discrepancies in Kirby's article passed unremarked.

"Penguin Panic"

Enter Mike Dash, a renowned British author/historian, Cambridge-educated in the mold of Ivan Sanderson, who spent twenty years as a contributing editor of *Fortean Times*. Toronto's *Globe and Mail* describes him as "that rarity: a perfectionist in his research and a writer who perfectly carves out his story with a pen as sharp as a stiletto." London's *Sunday Telegraph* calls Dash "an indefatigable researcher with a prodigious descriptive flair." The *New York Times* has praised his "unabashedly cinematic flair, backed by meticulous research."[19]

In 2000, Dash published *Borderlands,* billed as "The Ultimate Exploration of the Unknown." His chapter on hoaxes opens with Tony Signorini at Clearwater, but after briefly summarizing the events of 1948, Dash tells us that Signorini's lead boots "perfectly matched the plaster cast prints taken on Clearwater beach, proving that the affair was a hoax."[20] That fact was not revealed in Jan Kirby's original report from 1988—or anywhere else, prior to publication of *Borderlands*. Indeed, no photos of the forty-year-old casts were featured in the article detailing Signorini's statement, which displayed his homemade boots. Without a source we may be wise to ask whether the casts even survived to 1988, and if so, whether any "perfect match" was truly made.

Dash writes that "[w]hen the tracks were found it was observed that they seemed to have been made by a jointless, flat-bottomed foot." While that was true of some tracks, mostly found on public beaches, it does not describe those analyzed in Sanderson's report from 1948. As previously noted, those tracks featured flexible toes, prints with no visible ball or heel, and other traits clearly at odds with Signorini's alleged robotic leaping. Dash was not ignorant of Sanderson's report. In fact, he lists *More "Things"* as his primary source for the Clearwater case.[21]

Dash does acknowledge Sanderson's personal sighting of an unknown creature on the Suwannee River, but then writes: "The principal puzzle is how a naturalist of Sanderson's standing could have allowed himself to be taken in by what was really rather a crude deception."[22]

How "taken in"? By the evidence of his own eyes? By scientific calculations from a team of engineers?

Dash suggests: "Indeed, the existence of so many witnesses—Sanderson included—is extremely revealing. Given that there was no giant penguin haunting the Gulf Coast...what had [various witnesses] and the British naturalist actually seen? Another mystery animal, perhaps—but that seems to be stretching coincidence too far. It must be more likely that they had seen nothing at all, and either invented their stories out of mischief or to please their questioner, or caught up in the excitement of the giant penguin panic, misidentified known animals that they had glimpsed for only an instant. "[23]

But here's the rub: there was no "giant penguin panic" at Clearwater (or anywhere else) in 1948. As previously noted, Sanderson's penguin theory surfaced for the first time in *Fate* magazine, twenty years after the fact.[24] No one in Florida *expected* to see a giant penguin i 1948. They could not strive to "please their questioner" when no one asked about a penguir And indeed, none of the eyewitness descriptions recorded—including Sanderson's—referred to anything resembling a penguin, giant or otherwise.

As for Sanderson himself, it is likely that he lied about his sighting for "mischief's" sake and persuaded his pilot to join in the deception? No one questioned him, so a desire "to please" may be ruled out. Or was he grossly mistaken in what he saw, despite Dash's admission of his standing as a zoologist? More to the point, what creature known to science in the Sunshine State is twelve feet long and four feet wide, "domed above," with "things at either end" to churn up water? Wikipedia's suggestion that "some sharks might resemble a giant penguin when seen from above under adverse conditions" is farcical.[25]

As Dash reports, "The whole ridiculous business still retains the power to baffle."[26]

Plodding On

Another example of false information's proliferation surfaced in 2001, soon after the University Press of Florida published my own book of regional cryptid reports, *Florida's Unexpected Wildlife*. The book includes a chapter on Three-Toes, which examines Tony Signorini's tale. Soon after its release, one James Barrett-Morison reviewed the book online, reporting that the chapter in question describes "gigantic three-toed footprints stretching over twelve inches long, which appeared on the west coast of Florida between 1948 and 1958."[27] Barrett-Morison borrows the latter error from Jan Kirby's article of 11 June 1988, while shaving nearly two inches from the largest recorded footprints. Neither piece of misinformation appears in my text.

And so it goes.

On a slow news day in June 2006, reporter Jeff Klinkenberg resuscitated Tony Signorini's story for the *St. Petersburg Times*—and further muddied the waters. For starters, he seemingly had no idea when the events occurred, placing them "sixty years ago this summer," at a time when local residents enjoyed *The Big Sleep* at their local theater (released in 1946).[28]

Twelve paragraphs in, we discover that he's describing a preliminary "rampage" that supposedly took place a full year prior to the events on 1948, with Three-Toes traipsing around Indian Rocks, Sarasota, the Pinellas peninsula, St. Petersburg, and Tampa Bay (all sites listed by Jan Kirby for mythical track sightings between 1949 and 1958). No source available today supports these claims, but even if the incidents described by Klinkenberg did occur, he still has the year wrong.[29]

In 1948, Klinkenberg writes—avoiding a specific date—the creature "returned," surfacing near the mouth of the Suwannee River. He ignores its February premiere at Clearwater Beach and subsequent outings. While garbling the chronology beyond recognition, he also takes time out to slander Cambridge-educated Ivan Sanderson as "a self-taught zoologist," presumably incapable of distinguishing shite from Shinola.[30]

To cap his story, Klinkenberg collars Tony Signorini, then eighty-five years old, with a pocketful of rattling rosary beads to signify belated religious zeal. Church Tony blames the hoax on then-boss Al Williams, whose irrepressible sense of humor somehow left neighbors regarding him as "kind of crabby." Perhaps that was because his "jokes" ran toward such acts as locking horses up in jail and detonating explosive charges in the local fire station.[31]

What a card.

Signorini dates the Three-Toes hoax vaguely from 1946 or '47, when he was "about 25 or so." After that false start, his description of events jibes fairly well with his confession from June 1988: nocturnal forays, the bizarre leaping, and so on. This time around, he says, "I'm sure the police chief knew it was us, but he never said anything." Another brilliant wit, presumably. In closing, Klinkenberg suggests to Signorini that he launch a new monster flap. Tony's reply: "Sure, I'll go, though somebody will have to carry the monster shoes. They're too heavy for me now that I'm an old man."[31]

What finally remains of Tony Signorini's hoax confession? There is no doubt that he owned a pair of cast-lead "monster" feet in 1988. Whether he made the feet himself, or somehow got his hands on those fabricated by Sanderson's team forty years earlier—perhaps from friends in the police department who allegedly collaborated in his prank—remains unclear. No evidence exists that anyone has ever weighed the boots in question to discover whether they weigh thirty pounds or thirty-five, the recorded weight of Sanderson's models.

And beyond the lead boots ... nothing.

Unless Ivan Sanderson lied flagrantly about his Florida sighting and findings from 1948 to the end of his life, Signorini's story must be partly false, at least. Whether he faked some tracks or not, we know that Tony never weighed 4,000 pounds—the estimated bulk advanced by highway engineers for Three-Toes—and that rigid metal boots cannot show variation in their shape or size from one track to the next. It's physically impossible. If Signorini's boots made any tracks at all in Florida, they could not have produced the footprints analyzed by Sanderson.

Who was the hoaxer?

All we know today is that the mystery endures.

References

1.   Ivan Sanderson, *More "Things "* (New York: Pyramid Books, 1969), pp. 26-30.
2.   Ibid., p. 34.
3.   Ibid., p. 36.
4.   Ibid., p. 37.
5.   Ibid.
6.   Ibid., p. 43.
7.   Ibid.
8.   Ibid., pp. 50-1.
9.   Ibid., p. 50.
10.   Ibid., pp. 43, 45, 47, 51.
11.   Ibid. p. 30.
12.   Jan Kirby, "Clearwater Can Relax; Monster is Unmasked. " *St. Petersburg (FL) Times*, 11 June 1988.
13.   Ibid.
14.   Ibid.
15.   Ibid.
16.   Ibid.
17.   Ibid.
18.   Anonymous, "Florida 'Giant Penguin' Hoax Revealed, " *The ISC Newsletter* 7 (Winter 1988): 1-3.
19.   Mike Dash website, http://www.mikedash.com.
20.   Mike Dash, *Borderlands* (New York: Delta, 2000), p. 275.
21.   Ibid., pp. 275, 496; Sanderson, pp. 45-6.
22.   Dash, pp. 275.
23.   Ibid., pp. 274-5.
24.   Ivan Sanderson, "That Forgotten Monster: Old Three-Toes. " *Fate* 20 (December 1967): 66-75, and (January 1968): 85-93.
25.   "Giant penguin hoax," Wikipedia, http://en.wikipedia.org/wiki/Giant_penguin_hoax.
26.   Dash, p. 275.
27.   James Barrett-Morison, review of *Florida's Unexpected Wildlife*, Florida Book Review, http://www.floridabookreview.com/id34.html.
28.   Jeff Klinkenberg, "Man, not beast," *St. Petersburg Times*, 24 June 2006
29.   Ibid.
30.   Ibid.
31.   Ibid.
32.   Ibid.

4.
Bigfoot Just Died

Bluff Creek

Two events, nine years apart, largely define the public consciousness of Bigfoot/Sasquatch creatures in America. Neither begins nor ends the tale, but both are pivotal, intensely controversial, hedged with claims of hoaxes which, themselves, seem fabricated in an effort to deceive. The "mainstream" media has swallowed each successive claim in turn, without a hint of skeptical investigation, even when they contradict each other flatly, fatally.

The basic details of the first story are widely known, though often garbled in retelling. In spring 1957 contractor Raymond Wallace launched construction of a road at Bluff Creek, California. Raymond's brother Wilbur was the foreman, supervising a thirty-man team that included catskinner Gerald "Jerry" Crew (in charge of driving the heavy machinery). The crew completed ten miles of road before winter set in, then returned to the job in spring 1958.

According to later statements from Wilbur Wallace, trouble began at the worksite on 3 August 1958, when he found a 700-pound spare tire hurled into a gulch near the road. On 27 August, Jerry Crew reported finding huge humanoid footprints around his bulldozer. On 25 September the local *Humboldt Times* printed a letter penned by the wife of highway workman Jess Bemis, relating the crew's tales of "Big Foot." Jerry Crew found more tracks on 1 and 2 October, making plaster casts of some with help from tracker Bob Titmus. On 5 October, *Humboldt Times* columnist Andrew Genzoli published an article on "Bigfoot," including a photo of Crew with a footprint cast. On 12 October newly-hired workmen Bob Breaezle and Ray Kerr claimed a nocturnal Sasquatch sighting. Bob Titmus cast more prints at Bluff Creek on 1 November, later showing them to various researchers including René Dahinden, John Green, and millionaire monster-hunter Tom Slick. Before November's end, Slick organized a Pacific Northwest Expedition that pursued Bigfoot through much of 1959.[1]

The rest is history—and, as such, often misreported. For example, while Genzoli and the *Times* take credit for coining the nicknames "Big Foot" and "Bigfoot" for Sasquatch, the former was first used by residents of Rowan County, Kentucky, to describe a night-prowling manimal during the 1930s.[2]

Confusion also surrounds early claims of a hoax at Bluff Creek. Genzoli suggested a possible fraud in his original Bigfoot story, while the competing *Humboldt Standard* opined that the footprints were either a hoax or the trail of "a mentally deficient, over-grown boy gone wild." On 15 October 1958, *Times* reporter Bill Chambers told his readers that the Humboldt County sheriff had identified a prime suspect and expected a speedy confession. Said suspect—Ray Wallace—told the *Times*, "I'm not going in. If they want to put out a warrant I'm going to sue them for slander, and I won't fool around about it! If they think they're going to make a laughing stock out of me, they've got another thing [*sic*] coming."[3]

Tricksters

Today, we know that Wallace was, in fact, a hoaxer. Through the years, his claims regarding Bigfoot blossomed from fake tracks into fantasies suggesting that he may have lost his mind— or, at the very least, believed that others were crazy enough to believe him.

In February 1967 Wallace wrote to John Green, claiming discovery of an "ape cave" near Washington's Mount St. Helens, where creatures "have stayed for possibly several thousand years." In October 1969 he told California's *Klam-ity Kourier* that "Big Foot used to be very tame," accepting apples from Wallace and capering for films that brought Wallace offers of $250,000. In March 1970 he claimed possession of audio tapes, recorded while Sasquatches screamed and gobbled elderberries during "several hundred" encounters. May 1978 brought the assertion that "Big Footed creatures are people, they speak a language." Eleven months later, Wallace told John Green that "the Big Foots were killed and hauled down the Klamath River in a tug boat and out into the ocean 12 miles to where was a small ship anchored in international waters and frozen into a block of ice and then transported to Hong Kong and sold, so now there aren't any more left in northern California, or if there is they are being let out of flying saucers."[4]

In January 1981 Wallace advised the University of British Columbia that based on appearance, "I know that Big Foot and Sasquatches are all brothers or sisters." In the same letter, he claimed possession of film footage that showed a Sasquatch killing a deer. By then, he had also confessed faking tracks at Bluff Creek—but claimed it was part of a plan to save Bigfoot from hunters. The prints, Wallace said, were made with wooden feet he purchased from a friend for $50.[5]

Michael Dennett, head of Seattle's "Society for Sensible Explanations," identified Wallace's friend, more or less, in the autumn 1982 issue of *Skeptical Inquirer*. The culprit was eighty-six-year-old Rant Mullins (misspelled "Rent" by Dennett), whose marathon confession included claims that he and an accomplice staged the stoning of a Washington miner's cabin by "mountain devils" in July 1924, and that he started faking Sasquatch tracks with hand-carved wooden feet to "have some fun" in 1930. In all, Mullins claimed he had made eight separate pairs of ersatz monster feet, most of which "went to California." According to Mullins, however, his sale of wooden feet to Wallace occurred in 1969, when they met for the first time in Toledo, Washington.[6]

Exposure of Mullins failed to halt Wallace's antics. In December 1984 he offered John Green photos of a nine-foot male Sasquatch, but never delivered. In October 1989 he wrote to Green again, describing an alleged 1975 audience with "some government officials" who informed Wallace that "these big foots are being let out of flying saucers."[7] That absurdity did nothing to enhance his nonexistent credibility.

The bottom line: no serious Bigfoot researcher, from Tom Slick and Ivan Sanderson in 1959 to John Green thirty years later, ever took Ray Wallace seriously. Nor did the media.

That is, until he died.

A Liar's Legacy

Wallace gave up the ghost on 26 November 2002, at age eighty-four, in a Washington nursing home. Nine days later, an article in the *Seattle Times* quoted son Michael Wallace as saying, "Ray L. Wallace was Bigfoot. The reality is, Bigfoot just died."[8]

Two days later, the *Vancouver Sun* elaborated on the growing Wallace legend, crediting him with creating the beast depicted in Roger Patterson's famous Bigfoot film from October 1967 (see Chapter 5). According to the *Sun*, the film "was another of Wallace's fakes...he told Patterson where to go to spot the creature and knew who had been inside the suit." While the actor remained unnamed in print, the *Sun* declared that "most of the pictures of bigfoot...are in reality a hoaxer's wife dressed in a gorilla suit." That allegation flatly contradicted Michael Wallace, who told the *Seattle Times* that "his father called the Patterson film 'a fake' and said he had nothing to do with it."[9]

The *New York Times* treated Wallace to front-page coverage on 3 January 2003, and dished up more misinformation in the process. Reporter Timothy Egan led with a complaint from Michael Wallace that his father's hoax "was just a joke, and then it took on such a life of its own that even now, we can't stop it." Why not? Egan wrote: "Bigfoot defenders, including at least two scientists and a clinical psychologist who says he ran into the Big Guy two years ago in southern Oregon, are undeterred. They give Mr. Wallace credit for the hoax, which led to news stories around the world and began thousands of campfire debates. But, they say, other evidence is too strong to let a prank kill something that has become ingrained in the culture."[10]

Subsequently, all three authorities in question—Dr. Wolf Fahrenbach, retired from the Oregon Regional Primate Research Center; Dr. Jeffrey Meldrum, professor of anatomy and anthropology at Idaho State University; and Dr. Matthew Johnson, a clinical psychologist and Bigfoot witness—specifically refuted the words placed in their mouths by Egan. None gave Wallace "credit" for his hoaxes, and Dr. Meldrum specifically offered evidence refuting Wallace's claim that he hoaxed the tracks cast by Bob Titmus and others around Bluff Creek. None championed Bigfoot's existence as a cultural icon.[11]

Not that it mattered. By then, the hoax claim had indeed taken on a life of its own. CBS News belatedly boarded the bandwagon, playing it for laughs on 16 May 2003, as reporter Bill Whitaker asked Wallace's widow if she "knew Bigfoot intimately." "Oh, yes," Elna Wallace replied. "I slept with him."[12] An online Skeptics Dictionary floated the fantastic tale that, in addition to faking footprints, Wallace "also published photos and films of Bigfeet eating elk, frogs, and cereal."[13] In October 2008 the widow of *Humboldt Times* editor L. W. "Scoop" Beal claimed that her husband collaborated with Wallace in the original 1958 hoax. "It was just a fun thing and the fun got out of hand," she said.[14]

John Green and other researchers responded to the Wallace family's claims, but their replies were generally lost in the hilarity surrounding assertions that Wallace "created" or "invented" Bigfoot. That claim itself was preposterous, inasmuch as the first white settler's sighting of a hairy "wildman" in North America dates from 1785—133 years before Wallace was born[15]—but even that discrepancy can be explained, after a fashion.

Rising to defend the Wallace clan from "venomous denouncements," Internet blogger "Gian Quasar" wrote: "Despite John Green's association of the 'Bigfoot' with the Sasquatch, there is no similarity at all." In "Quasar's" view, identical descriptions spanning generations founder on the application of a different name.[16] In fact, however, Sasquatch was no more the legendary monster's "proper" name than Bigfoot: it was coined by Canadian journalist J. W. Burns in 1929.[17]

John Green himself responded to the Wallace claims by stating that "the tracks that were observed in the Bluff Creek drainage in northern California in the 1950's are not just another set of tracks that can easily be set aside as something tainted by claims of fakery." In Green's view, "The tracks at Bluff Creek appeared at a time and place when and where there was no knowledge of anything to imitate, circumstances that can never occur again." More specifically, he wrote, "Ray Wallace is connected to all this in only two ways that have been established. The men who first reported the 16" tracks were his employees, and it was the Bluff Creek events that started him on his long career, mainly after he moved to Washington, of producing and trying to sell crudely-faked track casts and photographs and telling outrageous whoppers about his adventures with 'Bigfoots.'"[18]

An endorsement of sorts for Green's view came, ironically, from *Strange Magazine* editor Mark Chorvinsky, described by the *Seattle Times* in 2002 as "one of the leading proponents of the theory that Mr. Wallace fathered Bigfoot." The *Times* quoted Chorvinsky as saying, "The fact is there was no Bigfoot in popular consciousness before 1958. America got its own monster, its own Abominable Snowman thanks to Ray Wallace."[19]

Still, for those in the know, there were claims of a big-footed beast at large, subject to imitation, long before 1958. Unless Rant Mullins lied outrageously—hardly impossible, for an admitted fraud—the hoaxing had begun in 1924, and Wallace was an upstart who began his trickery in 1969. Again, proof positive that Ray Wallace "invented" nothing.

Spokesmen for the Bigfoot Field Researchers Organization (BFRO) stand by Green's assertion that Wallace launched his career as a hoaxer well after the Bluff Creek events, and claims published in *Skeptical Inquirer* that the wooden feet displayed by Wallace relatives in 2002 "matched the Bluff Creek tracks" are refuted by various longtime researchers, with photographic comparisons to prove their point. Likewise, there is no evidence that any serious researcher was ever deceived by a Wallace hoax during the prankster's lifetime.[20]

Internet blogger Brian Dunning added a refreshing note of true skepticism to the Wallace case in 2006, when he wrote: "I see many cases on both sides of the Bigfoot debate where bad arguments, bad science, and just plain weirdness is being put forth, doing great disservice to their own side of the argument. There are intelligent and productive ways to explore a subject and present a case, but I don't see it being done very often on either side of the Bigfoot debate....Obviously, anyone who has any kind of basic understanding of research methodology can't accept Ray Wallace's story as proof that Bigfoot is a hoax. Sure, he made fake prints. So have a thousand other guys. They were doing it before Ray Wallace was born, and they're still doing it today. Anyone can be making those tracks. Anyone."[21]

Crypto-hoaxes may be driven by a range of motivations. While posthumous write-ups took pains to portray Ray Wallace as a "lovable trickster," Wallace also claimed possession of vast Bigfoot film footage—6,000 to 15,000 feet in some reports—and tossed around figures of $10,000 to $250,000 while hawking individual films or photos.[22] That said, no evidence has surfaced to suggest that any potential buyer ever took him seriously or paid Wallace a dime.

His survivors, however, may have done better.

At the peak of Wallace-Bigfoot fever, in early 2003, Reuters journalist Chris Gardner reported that actor Judge Reinhold (*Fast Times at Ridgemont High, Gremlins, Beverly Hills Cop,* etc.), wife Amy, and independent producer Eric Geadelmann had joined forces to create TLP Productions, with various movie projects in mind. According to Gardner, TLP had purchased rights to Wallace's life story for an undisclosed amount and planned two other films—a dark comedy titled *One Stupid Thing,* and a drama about the Ku Klux Klan called *Ghosts in the Hills.* Thus far, none of those films has been released, and a search of the Internet Movie Database on 30 June 2010 revealed no surviving trace of TLP Productions.[23]

The net result of Wallace mania was threefold. First—though sadly, not for the first time—it turned a spotlight on the media's capacity for swallowing wild tales, hook, line, and sinker. Throughout the feeding frenzy, only one American reporter—the *Denver Post*'s Theo Stein— showed anything resembling objectivity, with a front-page article that dismissed Wallace in a single line, while listing scientists—primatologists Jane Goodall and Russell Mittermeier; Esteban Sarmiento, functional anatomist with the American Museum of Natural History; Daris Swindler, emeritus professor of anthropology at the University of Washington; and George Schaller, international science director for the Wildlife Conservation Society—who agreed that "a hard-eyed look [at Bigfoot evidence] is absolutely essential."[24]

Sadly, for every Theo Stein there is a "Gian Quasar," telling the world that "There is no question that Ray Wallace was the Bigfoot." His proof? "Along with his brother he created the footprints in 1958, 1962, and 1967, which shows he was active for about 10 years in the area. One must only refer to the earliest books on the subject to see his wooden feet alone were the Bigfoot."[25]

Within a single paragraph, "Quasar" encapsulates the errors of the slightly better journalists who came before him. Seemingly unaware that Wallace left "the area"—i.e., Bluff Creek—in 1961, to settle in Toledo, Washington, "Quasar" proceeds to credit Ray with various California track finds and films spanning the next six years. His argument collapses totally with the reference to early Bigfoot books (or any others, for that matter), which display Sasquatch footprint casts bearing no resemblance to Wallace's crude wooden feet, in either shape or size. Ironically, "Quasar" himself provides a hand-drawn "fatal comparison for Bluff Creek," revealing that Wallace's boots and the footprints discovered had nothing in common.[26]

Was Ray Wallace a hoaxer, for whatever motive? Absolutely.

Did he bamboozle any serious Bigfoot researchers? Absolutely not.

He neither "invented" nor personified Bigfoot. His passing ended nothing but a life of lies. And if he was responsible for all the Bigfoot-Yeti tracks reported from five continents from 1958 until his death, he must have presided over a global conspiracy dwarfing the CIA and KGB combined.

The mystery endures.

References

1.   The chronology is summarized from Loren Coleman's *Bigfoot! The True Story of Apes in America* (New York: Paraview, 2003), pp. 66-71, and John Green's *Sasquatch: The Apes Among Us* (Blaine, WA: Hancock House, 1978), pp. 65-82.
2.   Michael Newton, *Strange Kentucky Monsters* (Atglen, PA: Schiffer, 2010), p. 53.
3.   John Driscoll, "Birth of Bigfoot," *The Times-Standard* (Eureka, CA), 30 October 2008.
4.   "Wallace Hoax Behind Bigfoot?" Bigfoot Field Researchers Organization (BFRO), http://www.bfro.net/news/wallace.asp#commentarY.
5.   Ibid.; Coleman, pp. 76-7.
6.   Michael Dennett, "Bigfoot Jokester Reveals Punch Line—Finally," *Skeptical Inquirer* 7 (Fall 1982): 8-9.
7.   BFRO, "Wallace Hoax Behind Bigfoot?"
8.   Bob Young, "Lovable trickster created a monster with Bigfoot hoax," *Seattle Times*, 5 December 2002.
9.   "Footprints big but 42-year Bigfoot hoax even larger," *Vancouver Sun*, 7 December 2002; Young.
10.   Timothy Egan, "Search for Bigfoot Outlives The Man Who Created Him," *New York Times*, 3 January 2003.
11.   BFRO, "Wallace Hoax Behind Bigfoot?"

12. "Bigfoot Remains Mysterious," CBS Evening News with Dan Rather, (16 May 2003), http://www.encyclopedia.com/doc/1P1-74033087.html.
13. "Bigfoot," The Skeptics Dictionary, http://www.skepdic.com/bigfoot.html.
14. Driscoll.
15. Chad Arment, *The Historical Bigfoot* (Landisville, PA: Coachwhip, 2006), p. 187.

16. Gian Quasar, "On the Trail of the Sasquatch: Exposing the truth about Bigfoot," http://www.bermuda-triangle.org/html/bluff_creek_bigfoot.html.

17. Michael Newton, *Encyclopedia of Cryptozoology* (Jefferson, NC: McFarland, 2005), p. 412.

18. "John Green's Commentary of the 'Birth of Bigfoot' Story." BFRO, http://www.bfro.net/news/jgreen_bluff_creek_tracks.asp.

19. Young.

20. "BFRO's Quick FAQ on the 12/02 'Death of Bigfoot' Story," BFRO, http://www.bfro.net/news/wallace_faq.asp; Joe Nickell, "Mysterious Entities of the Pacific Northwest, Part I," *Skeptical Inquirer* 31 (January/February 2007), http://www.csicop.org/si/show/mysterious_entities_of_the_pacific_northwest_part_i.

21. Brian Dunning, "Killing Bigfoot with Bad Science," *Skeptoid* 11 (3 December 2006), http://skeptoid.com/episodes/4011.

22. "New Bigfoot Photo Investigation," *Strange Magazine* 13 (Spring 1994), http://www.bigfootencounters.com/articles/strange14.htm.

23. Chris Gardner, "Reinholds put their Bigfoot forward in venture," Reuters/Hollywood Reporter, at BFRO, http://www.bfro.net/news/wallace.asp#producers.

24. Theo Stein, "Bigfoot Believers: Legitimate scientific study of legend gains backing of top primate experts," *Denver Post*, 5 January 2003.

25. Quasar.

26. Ibid.

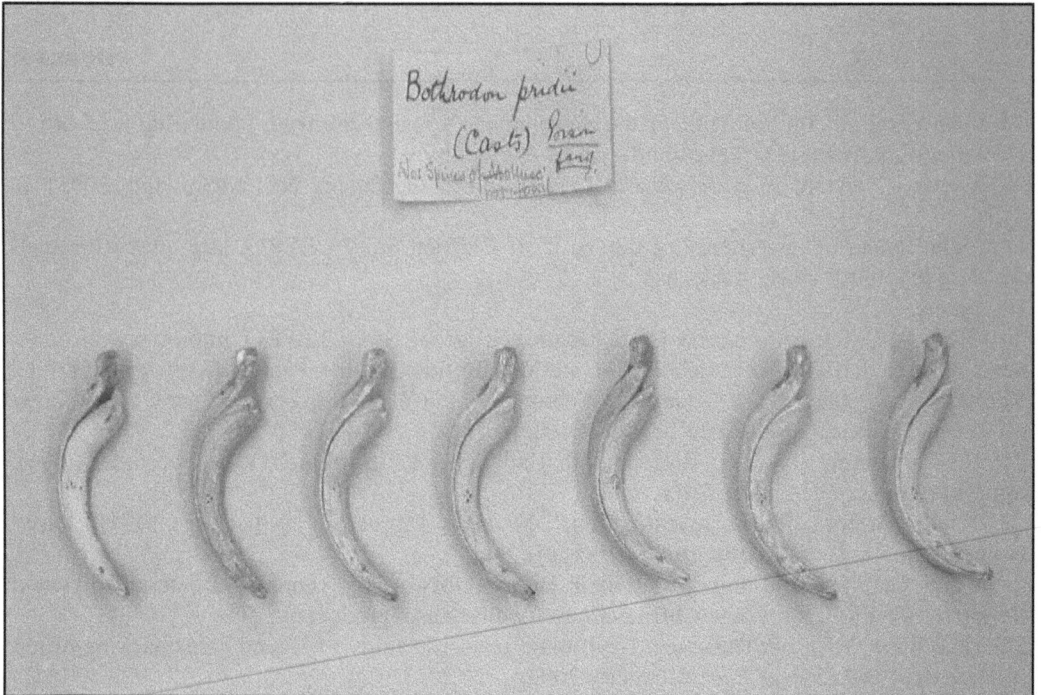

Casts made from the supposed fossil fang of a giant prehistoric viper, *Bothrodon pridii*, later proved to be part of a seashell.

"Fragrant Flower," the Indonesian reticulated python originally advertised in 2003 as being 50 feet long.

A WESTERN WHAT IS IT?

A Mysterious Creature in British Columbia.

The village of Yale, B. C., is situated at the head of navigation on Fraser River, ninety miles above New Westminster, which was the capital of British Columbia until it was changed to Victoria. About twenty miles from Yale, on the line of the railroad, is a locality roughly known as "Tunnel No. 4," where the extraordinary occurrence about to be related took place during the early part of the present month.

Notwithstanding the improbability of any amount of prospecting resulting in turning up even the bones of the "missing link," much less in finding an actual living specimen of this much debated being, the actual facts which are related concerning the remarkable appearance near "Tunnel No. 4" would tend to bear out this theory of the subject. At different times during the past two years there has been seen in the hilly country about the settlements a being whose personal appearance is variously described.

One day about a year ago a party of young people from Yale went up on the road as far as Tunnel No. 4, and there, disembarking from the cars, proceeded to spread themselves over the country in the form of a picnic party. The tempting meal had been spread upon the ground, and young men and girls were seated in a circle preparing to enjoy the viands, when there was heard a loud crashing noise above their heads, and in an instant, without further warning than was given by a most fiendish yell—something between the shriek of a hyena and the Indian war whoop—there dropped into the midst of the spread a horrible creature as large as a man, covered with hair from head to foot, with long arms which he brandished about in formidable style, as he vainly tried to extricate himself from the canned fruits, cold meats, jam pots, and oleomargarine into which he had unexpectedly tumbled. This was a "surprise party" for which no intentional preparation had been made, and in a moment there was a stampede.

Tumbling headlong down the hill on whose crest the elaborate meal had been laid, the frightened picknickers so hastened their departure as to be utterly unable to give any coherent description of what had frightened them to the railroad men whose assistance they implored. A party fully armed was at once made up, and the scene of the sudden onslaught was carefully approached. The unwelcome visitor had fled, but before leaving he had plainly helped himself to everything that took his fancy, and that seemed to have been guided by nothing but the opportunity. If he were a human creature and had eaten what was certainly gone, selected from every imaginable article of food, his remains would undoubtedly be found in a few hours. No idiot Indian or other kind of man could possibly have eaten such a mixture and live.

But if such was the case, the most careful search failed to result in finding the body, and after a protracted search, which lasted, after a desultory fashion, for several weeks, the idea of his having died of indigestion or gout was reluctantly abandoned. One fact which was demonstrated by the circumstances of this visitation caused the believers in the Indian theory to be very deeply shaken in their convictions. This was that he had fallen from an overhanging limb of a tree, carrying a large piece with him, and the size of the limb was a good indication that the creature must be as heavy as an ordinary sized man, and hardly an Indian, as they do not usually climb trees. A few months later another view of this strange being was had by some workmen on the railroad, but, though they gave chase, they were not able to come up with him. He was not seen again until about three weeks ago, when he was not only seen, but caught. The spot where he was discovered was a series of bluffs, deemed inaccessible. A train was running from Lytton to Yale, when the engineer saw what he supposed to be a man lying close to the track. He whistled down brakes, but just as the train stopped the object sprang to its feet, and in an instant the object was climbing the side of the precipitous declivity with the greatest ease. The conductor, brakemen, express messenger, and a number of passengers at once gave chase, and after some perilous climbing succeeded in corralling the creature on an overhanging shelf of rock from which he could neither ascend nor descend. The ingenious, though rather cruel, method was now adopted for securing him, of dropping a piece of stone from above, which, falling on his head, stunned him, and he fell insensible.

The bell rope was now procured, and, after some expert climbing, he was reached, tied, and lowered gradually down to the foot of the cliff. He was placed in the baggage car and successfully transported to Yale, when it was found that he had recovered from his insensibility, and was tractable and docile. One of the men in the railroad machine shop assumed the care of him, named him Jacko, and very soon made his friendly acquaintance. And even then, and up to the present time, it has not been satisfactorily ascertained to what race the new discovery belongs. He is of the gorilla type, but not definitely enough to be declared a gorilla, which is, moreover, a creature unknown to the latitude of British Columbia—while there has been no menagerie there to introduce even a monkey. He is about 4 feet 7 inches in height, and weighs 127 pounds. His entire body, except his hands and feet, is covered with black, glossy hair about one inch in length, but his forearm is much longer than that of a man, and so strong that he will break a stick—by wrenching or twisting it—so large that no man could possibly accomplish this feat. He makes a noise, half bark and half growl, but is generally quiet. His favorite food is berries, and he drinks fresh milk with evident relish. His captor intends taking him to London for exhibition. Then his exact position in natural history will probably be discovered.

Hoaxed newspaper coverage of "Jacko," a juvenile Sasquatch reportedly captured in British Columbia.

The "Loch Ness tooth"—actually a deer's antler—employed in a 2005 literary publicity stunt.

Bigfoot photos amaze experts

By DICK DONOVAN

An amazing series of pictures that captured a Bigfoot bathing in a mountain stream is the first conclusive proof that the legendary creature of the wilds really lives!

The monster emerges from brush (top)

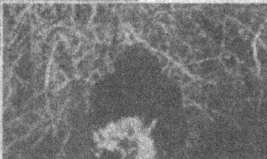

Dubious Bigfoot photos published by Tom Biscardi years before the Georgia carcass hoax of 2008.

Dr. DeWitt Webb with the St. Augustine "globster" of 1896.

Workmen attempting to move the Florida globster farther inland.

Another view of the St. Augustine carcass.

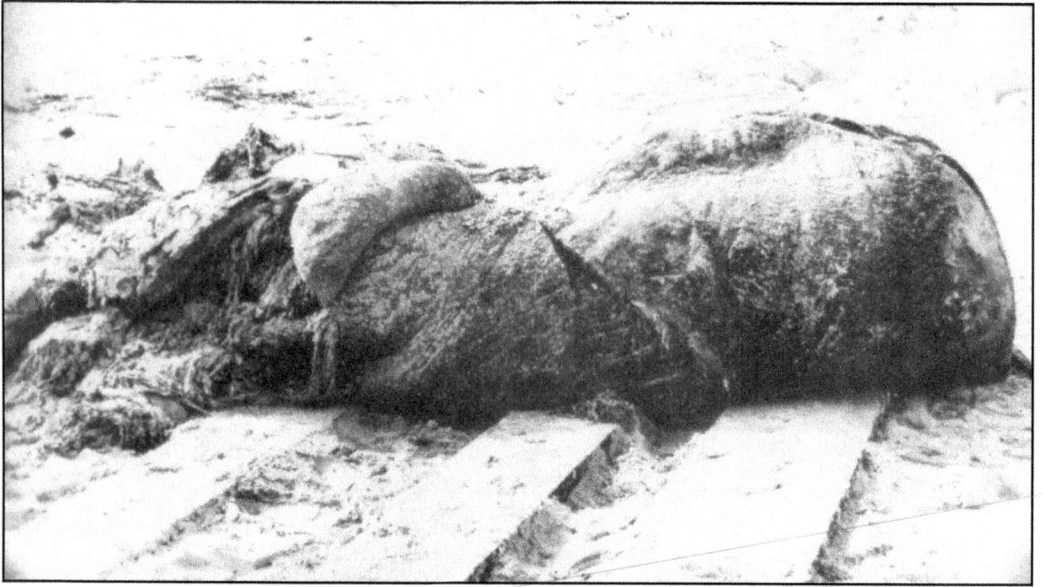

The carcass photographed from a different angle.

A sketch of the carcass by Dr. Webb, illustrating its size and apparent truncated arms.

Another Webb sketch of the Florida globster.

Dr. Addison Verrill, who "debunked" Octopus giganteus from a distance of 900 miles.

A. E. Verrill

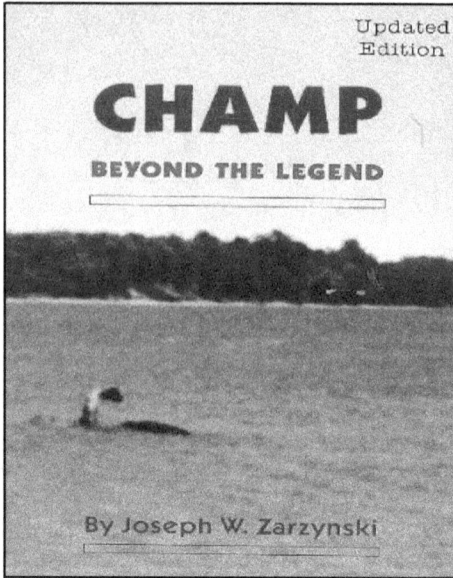

Joseph Zarzynski's book on "Champ,"
displaying Sandra Mansi's photo as
its cover illustration.

A monument to Champ and witnesses who have reported sightings.

Champ serves as mascot for a Minor League Baseball team, the Vermont Lake Monsters.

Ivan Sanderson prepared a detailed report on Florida's three-toed footprints in 1948.

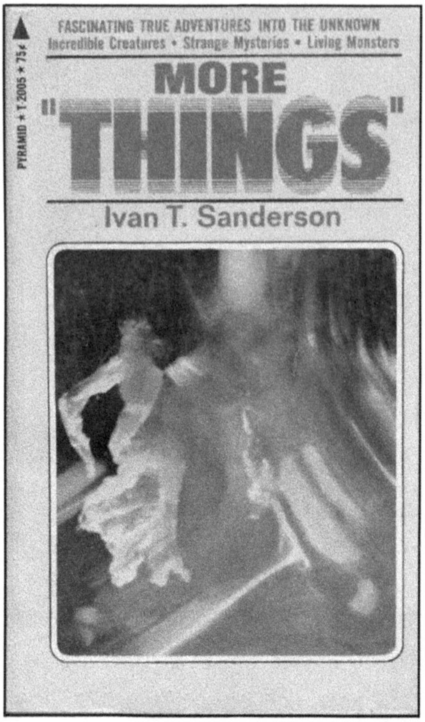

PYRAMID • T-2005 • 75¢
FASCINATING TRUE ADVENTURES INTO THE UNKNOWN
Incredible Creatures • Strange Mysteries • Living Monsters
MORE
"THINGS"
Ivan T. Sanderson

Sanderson's speculation on a giant penguin was not published until 1968, then reprinted in More "Things" the following year.

BELOW: Newspaper coverage of Bigfoot tracks found at Bluff Creek, California, in October 1958.

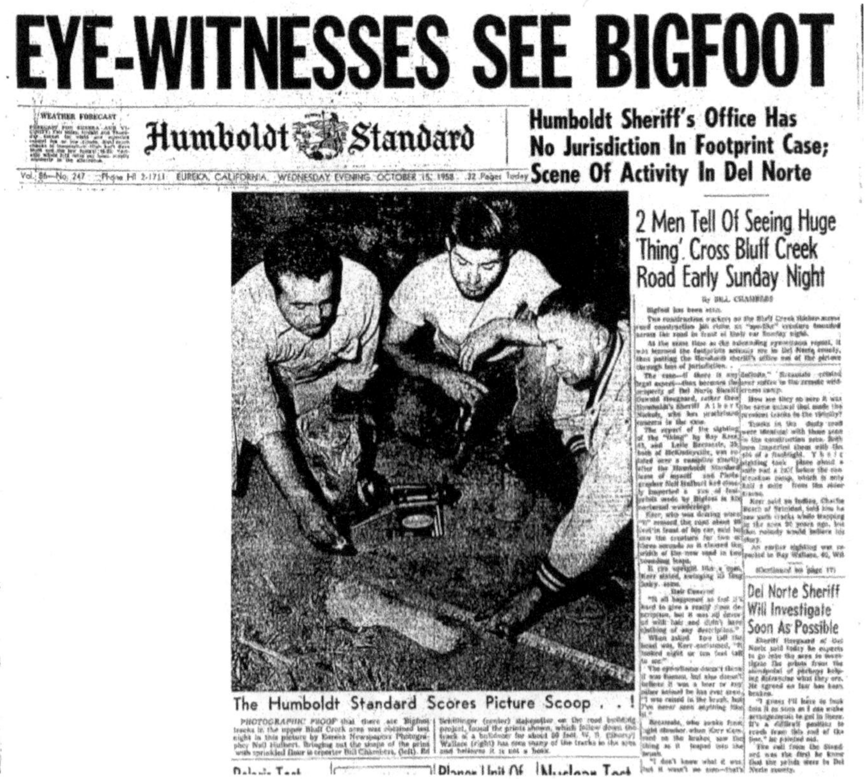

EYE-WITNESSES SEE BIGFOOT

WEATHER FORECAST

Humboldt Standard

Vol. 86—No. 247 Phone HI 2-1711 EUREKA, CALIFORNIA, WEDNESDAY EVENING, OCTOBER 15, 1958 32 Pages Today

Humboldt Sheriff's Office Has No Jurisdiction In Footprint Case; Scene Of Activity In Del Norte

2 Men Tell Of Seeing Huge 'Thing'. Cross Bluff Creek Road Early Sunday Night

By BILL CHAMBERS

Bigfoot has been seen.

Del Norte Sheriff Will Investigate Soon As Possible

The Humboldt Standard Scores Picture Scoop . . !

Raymond Wallace, the "lovable trickster" who faked various footprints and offered nonexistent Bigfoot films for sale at exorbitant prices.

A still frame of "Patty" from the Patterson film of October 20, 1967.

Roger Patterson—"genius" hoaxer, or the man who caught Sasquatch on film?

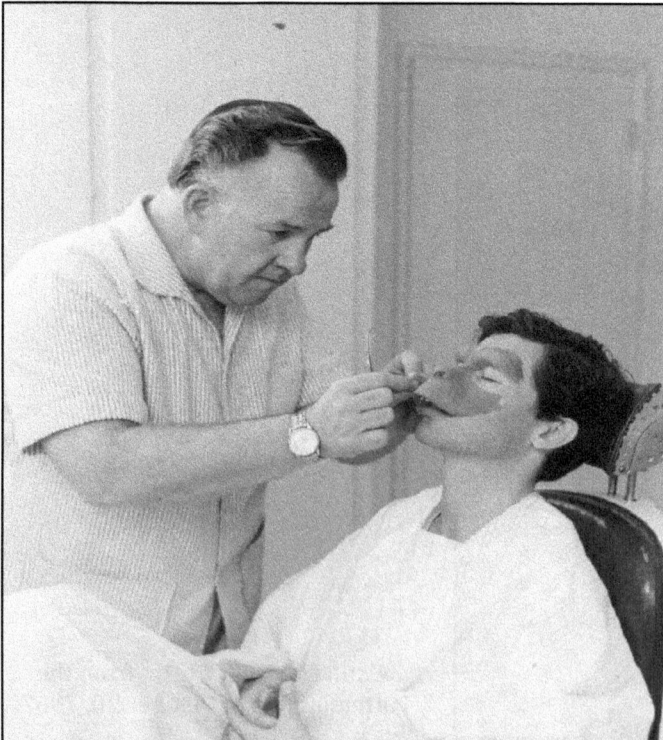

John Chambers, seen applying makeup to an actor for *Planet of the Apes* in 1968, denied any role in the Patterson film.

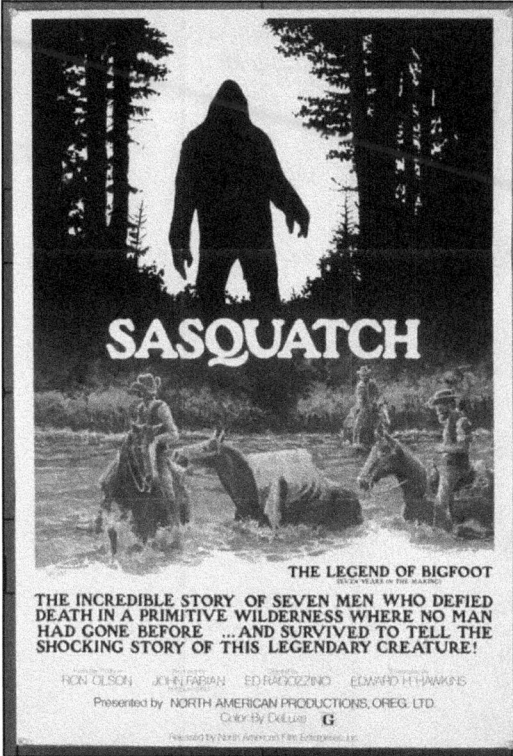

A poster for the Bigfoot film released by American National Enterprises in 1977, five years after Roger Patterson's death.

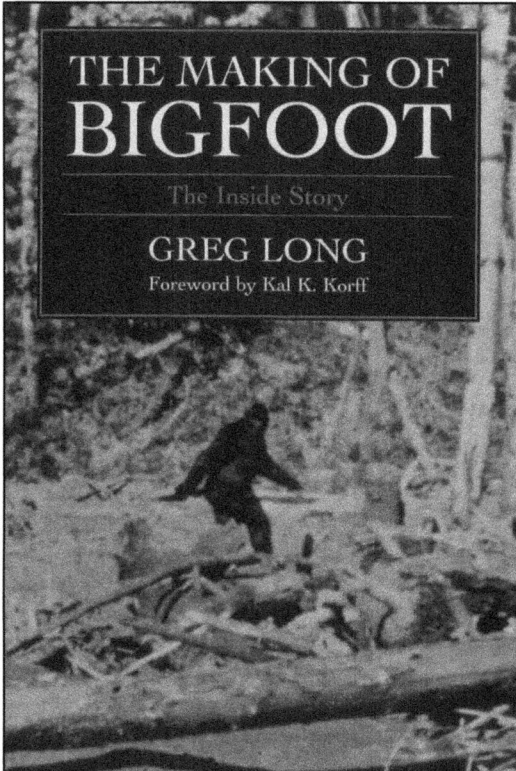

Greg Long's "monster book" on the Patterson film.

M. A. WETHERELL.
Photo by O'Byrne

Marmaduke Wetherell, photographed in 1916.

The "surgeon's photo" of Nessie, as published on 21 April 1934.

Dr. Wilson's second controversial photograph.

The uncropped "surgeon's photo" still reveals no foreground
or significant background features.

Steuart Campbell recovered the uncropped Wilson photo from obscurity in 1984.

CAMERA PROVES LOCH NESS SEA SERPENT IS JUST A WHALE

By IDENTIFYING the sea serpent of Loch Ness, Scotland, as a familiar species of whale, naturalists have just shown how easily the human eye may be fooled into thinking it sees an unfamiliar monster. Worldwide interest was drawn to Loch Ness, within recent months, by repeated eyewitness reports of a long-necked, aquatic apparition of huge size, resembling no known marine animal. Finally Dr. Robert K. Wilson, noted British surgeon, managed to get a snapshot of the fabulous creature, and the mystery vanished. The picture showed the curved fin of a killer whale projecting in typical fashion from the water strongly suggesting an elongated neck and head. According to Dr. Roy Chapman Andrews, noted explorer and zoologist, and others who agreed on this identification, the whale evidently had strayed up an inlet from the sea into the lake. This was the second sea monster mystery to be cleared up recently. Examination showed a strange marine creature, washed up dead on French shores near Cherbourg (P.S.M., May, '34, p. 38), to be a basking shark of a common species, made almost unrecognizable by the waves.

Left, first photo of the Loch Ness sea serpent which apparently had a head and neck protruding above the water. Below, arrow points to curved fin of killer whale which is out of the water as whale swims. The sea serpent was just a whale

One of many articles attempting to explain the Wilson photo's subject as a known animal, claiming that it depicts an orca.

Nessie hunt goes on after scientists concede hoax

By JOHN YOUNG

A SCIENTIST investigating the existence of the Loch Ness monster refused to dismiss the popular legend yesterday, in spite of the most famous picture of the supposed creature being exposed as a hoax.

Adrian Shine, leader of the Loch Ness and Morar Project, set up to discover whether a mysterious being inhabits the deep waters southwest of Inverness, even welcomed the revelation that the photograph which appeared in the Daily Mail in April 1934 was a fraud.

According to new claims, the picture was concocted using a toy submarine fitted with the head and neck of a sea serpent made from plastic wood. It was taken by Colonel Robert Wilson, a Harley Street gynaecologist, who claimed to have seen "something in the water" on April 19, 1934, and has since been known as the Surgeon's Photograph.

Researchers have, however, discovered that Wilson was the front man for a conspiracy to hoodwink Fleet Street led by Marmaduke Wetherell, a self-styled big

game hunter, who had been hired by the Daily Mail to track down the monster. The other members of the group were Wetherell's son Ian, his stepson Christian Spurling, and Maurice Chambers, an insurance broker, all of whom are now dead.

Wetherell is said to have been motivated by revenge after his "discovery" of footprints on a beach in Loch Ness was discredited by the Natural History Museum, which said the prints had been made by the dried foot of a hippopotamus, perhaps part of an umbrella stand.

Mr Shine said yesterday

that he was convinced that the report of the hoax was valid. Much of the research was carried out by one of his own staff, Alastair Boyd. "It was always a very controversial photograph," he said. When the negative was inspected, the "monster" was found to be very small.

But Mr Shine added: "Eyewitness acounts still suggest that there is something powerful in the loch. As scientists, we naturally resent hoax evidence, because it discredits the seriousness of our research. I hope the whole mystery can now be approached more openly."

Hoaxers: Marmaduke Wetherell and Colonel Wilson

The Surgeon's Photograph is now said to show a fake Nessie made of plastic wood

Newspaper coverage of the 1994 Spurling hoax "exposé."

Mock Ness Monster

Was the beast in that famous snap just a toy submarine from Woolworth's?

By JOHN WOODCOCK

IT looked like flesh and blood ... but was it just plastic wood?

For 60 years, this celebrated 1934 photograph of a long-necked creature popping its head above water (right) has helped keep afloat the legend of the Loch Ness Monster.

After scientific tests on the film, even sceptics were convinced there was nothing fishy about the creature. It seemed irrefutable evidence that something strange was flapping about out there.

But now, it is claimed, it was all a monstrous hoax . . . and Nessie's money-spinning credibility could be about to take a nosedive.

The creature in the film is said to be nothing more than a 1ft high plastic wood model, painted grey. It was powered not by a pair of huge flippers, but by a clockwork toy submarine bought for a few shillings from Woolworth's.

The 1934 picture became known as the Surgeon's Photograph, because it was attributed to Colonel Robert Wilson, a Harley Street gynaecologist who claimed to have recorded "something in the water" on April 19 that year. Now it is alleged he was part of a plot to perpetuate the myth of the monster which began as a joke but rapidly spun out of control.

One of the pranksters, Christian Spurling — who died last November aged 90 — allegedly confessed the whole thing to Loch Ness researchers David Martin and Alastair Boyd.

Christian was the stepson of the man at the centre of the hoax, Marmaduke Weatherell — who also

recruited his son Ian, and insurance broker Maurice Chambers.

Weatherell wanted revenge after being ridiculed over footprints of the 'monster' he had found on a beach at Loch Ness the previous year. They turned out to have been made by a dried hippo foot — perhaps part of an umbrella stand.

Christian, an expert modelmaker, said that in January 1933 his

stepfather asked him: 'Can you make me a monster?'

The creature was created in eight days and underwent sea trials on a pond before being taken to Loch Ness to be photographed. Four snaps were then given to Colonel Wilson, who already had his story prepared.

The picture — first published in the Daily Mail — caused a sensation. But the pranksters were so overwhelmed

by the deluge of publicity that they decided not to divulge the truth.

Today, all those involved are dead, but the legacy of what they unwittingly created lives on. The Nessie legend attracts thousands of visitors a year to the 23-mile long, 750ft deep loch plus a steady stream of researchers. It is one of the most important industries in the Highlands, generating an estimated £25million a year from tourism.

The nearby village of Drumnadrochit is home to the Official Loch Ness Monster Exhibition, which has made its owner, Ronnie Bremner, a millionaire.

And the Government's marketing agency, Highlands and Islands Enterprise, unashamedly exploits Nessie to promote the area as a holiday venue.

Was it real, or did deceit raise its ugly head? Top left: The 1934 picture. Above: How the model monster may have been made

Yesterday, its spokesman was undismayed by the latest dent to the monster's credibility. 'The legend has been with us since the sixth century and I can't see its popularity being harmed by yet another controversy,' he said. 'Tourists don't just come here to try to get a glimpse of Nessie. They're attracted by the scenery as much as by the intrigue of what may or not be in the loch. Where Nessie's concerned, all publicity is good publicity.'

Exhibition boss Mr Bremner was also taking it philosophically. 'We show the picture, but don't claim it is genuine,' he said. 'The fact that it may have been proved a fake will not damage the show's popularity, but strengthen it. There are countless other pieces of evidence pointing to a large beast inhabiting the loch.'

More media coverage of the "hoax," ignoring its many inconsistencies.

NESSIE

THE SURGEON'S PHOTOGRAPH

David Martin and Alastair Boyd

The "hoax" revisited by David Martin and Alastair
Boyd, five years after its initial publication.

5.
Patty Whacked

Patty's Close-up

As we have just passed the forty-sixth anniversary of the Patterson film, purportedly depicting a Sasquatch in the wilds of northern California, it is instructive to review the several conflicting "revelations" of a hoax behind those striking images. This chapter is not intended to support the film's legitimacy. That case has been argued in intricate detail by the late Dr. Grover Krantz[1] and Dr. Jeffrey Meldrum[2], among others. Rather, as in prior chapters, we shall examine the nature of hoax claims advanced by professional debunkers, and the mainstream media's reaction to those claims.

The story of the Patterson film is too well known to require detailed recitation here. On 20 October 1967, Bigfoot-hunters Roger Patterson and Bob Gimlin claimed an encounter with a female Sasquatch near Bluff Creek, California—site of the footprint discovery which gave "Bigfoot" its popular media nickname nine years earlier (see Chapter 4). Patterson captured his subject on 952 frames of 16mm film, which subsequently eclipsed the 1934 "surgeon's photo" of Nessie (see Chapter 6) as a photographic icon among cryptozoology buffs. Some unknown viewer dubbed the creature "Patty," after Patterson.

Opinions concerning the film were then—and remain today—starkly, even bitterly, divided. Patterson's footage was, as author Daniel Perez opined, "the Zapruder film" of Sasquatch research.[3] Debates surrounding it include the camera's filming speed, its distance from the subject, circumstances of the film's development—and, naturally, whether or not the film itself is a fake. Largely ignored or dismissed out of hand without viewing by major scientific institutions, the Patterson film has nonetheless been subjected to repeated, detailed scrutiny, with mixed results.

Burbank Bigfoot

Anthropologist David Daegling noted the relatively primitive state of Hollywood special effects in 1967, concluding that if the film depicted a costumed actor, "it is not unreasonable to suggest that it is better than some of the tackier monster outfits that got thrown together for television at that time."[4] Grover Krantz, Jeffrey Meldrum, and Dmitri Donskoy—chief of the biomechanics department at the Soviet Union's Central Institute of Physical Culture, later affiliated with Moscow's Darwin Museum—all concluded that the film portrayed a nonhuman subject.[5]

Contrary opinions were also recorded. Late *Strange Magazine* publisher Mark Chorvinsky claimed, without citing a source, that Bernard Heuvelmans—the "Father of Cryptozoology " and proponent of a theory that yetis are relict Neandertals—rejected the Patterson film as a hoax.[6] Primatologist John Napier, though persuaded of Bigfoot's existence by deformed footprints from Washington State, declared, "There is little doubt that the scientific evidence taken collectively points to a hoax of some kind. The creature shown in the film does not stand up well to functional analysis." Still, he added: "I could not see the zipper; and I still can't. There I think we must leave the matter. Perhaps it was a man dressed up in a monkey-skin; if so it was a brilliantly executed hoax and the unknown perpetrator will take his place with the great hoaxers of the world. Perhaps it was the first film of a new type of hominid, quite unknown to science, in which case Roger Patterson deserves to rank with Dubois, the discoverer of *Pithecanthropus erectus*, or Raymond Dart of Johannesburg, the man who introduced the world to its immediate human ancestor, *Australopithecus africanus*."[7]

First suspicions of a hoax naturally focused on Roger Patterson and Bob Gimlin. Patterson published a book on Bigfoot in 1966 and made no secret of his desire to capture the cryptid on film. Gimlin apparently signed on as a hired hand, and in some accounts remains bitter today at being cheated out of hypothetical profits. Still, the question remains: did either man—or both, acting in concert—have the requisite funds, knowledge, or skill to produce a realistic movie monster?

Roger Patterson claimed that he showed his film to unnamed experts "in the special effects department at Universal Studios in Hollywood," who allegedly told him, "We could try [duplicating it], but we would have to create a completely new system of artificial muscles and find an actor who could be trained to walk like that. It might be done, but we would have to say that it would be almost impossible."[8] Longtime researcher Peter Byrne reportedly showed the film to five animation experts at Disney Studios, who called it "a beautiful piece of work" but opined that it must have been shot in a studio.[9]

Grover Krantz, although committed to the film's authenticity, declared that Patterson "might have tried to fake a film of this kind if he had the ability to do so," but in Krantz's judgment, based on long acquaintance with Patterson, "he had nowhere near the knowledge or facilities to do so—nor, for that matter, had anyone else."[10] David Daegling agreed, reporting that "most acquaintances of Patterson volunteered that neither he nor Gimlin were clever enough to put something that detailed together."[11]

In which case, who might be responsible?

Mark Chorvinsky volunteered the first of several contradictory answers in the summer 1996 issue of *Strange Magazine*. A longtime professional magician—and a self-styled "expert in creating hoaxes"[12]—Chorvinsky told his readers that the ape suit worn by some unknown actor in Patterson's film was created by Hollywood makeup artist John Chambers, whose work graced films ranging from *Around the World in Eighty Days* (1956) to *Class Reunion* (1982). More relevant was Chambers's work creating ape masks for *Planet of the Apes* and two sequels during 1968-72.[13]

Chorvinsky's sources included various Hollywood insiders, some still anonymous today. Among those he identified, Chorvinsky quoted makeup artists John Vulich and Mike McCracken Sr. to document Chambers's creation of an ape costume for the TV series *Lost in Space*, a "revelation" that was news to no one except, oddly enough, one Flint Mitchell, described by Chorvinsky as "a *Strange Magazine* reader and the head of a *Lost in Space* fan club." Asked by Chorvinsky to speculate on "the notion that the Patterson suit may have been modified from a *Lost in Space* costume," Mitchell deemed it "entirely possible."[14] His evidence or first-hand knowledge: nonexistent.

Next, "*Strange Magazine* subscriber Tim Johnson also offered his help on the investigation." That "help" consisted of surmising that Chambers created "giant, hairy mutant" costumes for several *Lost in Space* episodes which—we know today, thanks to online archives—included no work by Chambers. Chorvinsky then watched those irrelevant programs with *Strange Magazine* executive editor Douglas Chapman and art director Greg Snook, who agreed with their boss, more or less, that something was up. Even then, however, Snook noted that "We never see any of the monsters in the same pose as in the Patterson film, making it very hard to compare the creatures"—which Chambers didn't create, in the first place. Indeed, Chorvinsky himself finally concluded that makeup men Tom Burman and Janos Prohaska "may have been responsible for the *Lost in Space* monsters, not Chambers."[15]

Moving on from that dead-end, Chorvinsky floated a claim that "for years it has been 'generally known' in the Hollywood special effects makeup community that Academy Award winning makeup artist John Chambers fabricated the suit in the Patterson Bigfoot film." After all, we're told, Chambers created the makeup for *Planet of the Apes* in 1967 (released to theaters in 1968). Ignoring the fact that said makeup consisted only of masks, gloves, and feet, with no full-body costumes, Chorvinsky hedged his bets, writing: "Whether Chambers created the suit or not, it is highly significant that so many makeup artists believe the film to be a hoax."[16]

And who were they? Among "a number of the top makeup people in Hollywood," Chorvinsky identified the following:

Screenwriter/director/producer Donald Glut—involved in thirty-seven films since 1965[17]—who allegedly told "*Strange Magazine* reader Alex Downs" that he (Glut) "heard about Chambers making the suit."[18]

Animatronics expert David Kindlon, who heard the Chambers rumor second-hand from makeup artists Howard Berger and Rick Baker, but possessed no first-hand knowledge.[19]

Howard Berger, who repeated the tale to Chorvinsky, citing Rick Baker as his source. When asked how Baker knew the "facts," Berger explained, "He probably heard it from John Chambers, that's what I figure."[20]

Baker himself declined Chorvinsky's requests for an interview, leaving Chorvinsky disappointed but free to speculate that "it is highly significant that Baker believed the film to be a fake. He, if anyone, would know."[21] Baker's silence, of course, proves precisely nothing.

Actor Bob Burns, described by the Internet Movie Database as a "world renown [*sic*] archivist and historian of props, costumes, and other screen used paraphernalia"—yet relegated by Chorvinsky to the status of an "ape impersonator"—was vague in the extreme. Concerning the Chambers rumor, he told Chorvinsky, "I don't remember where I heard it from, but I didn't hear it from Rick [Baker] at all, as a matter of fact. It is generally known in the special effects business here, that it's kind of common knowledge that the film footage was faked by John Chambers."[22]

Jon Vulich named FX artist Bart Mixon and makeup specialist Jim McPherson as third-hand sources for the Chambers tale, but Chorvinsky cited no interviews with either, though both are apparently still living.[23]

Matt Croteau, identified by Chorvinsky as "a makeup sculptor and *Strange Magazine* reader," told Chorvinsky that "he had heard from reputable sources that friends and relatives of Chambers knew that he worked on the Patterson suit. This information originated from a source very close to John Chambers. Croteau's sources have chosen to remain nameless but I [Chorvinsky] know who they are."[24] And they deserve the same respect as any other third-hand anonymous witness—whose claims, as we shall see, were flatly denied by Chambers himself.

Makeup master Tom Burman, a close associate of Chambers in the 1960s, told Chorvinsky flatly, "Naw, he didn't make that suit. One, he wouldn't have made a suit that bad, and number two, I knew him during that time and in '67 we were doing *Planet of the Apes*, so we would have had no time to do a suit."[25]

Understandably frustrated, Chorvinsky preferred the story told by "a prominent makeup artist who prefers to remain anonymous." That source not only branded Burman a liar, but also claimed "that Tom Burman was allegedly the person in the Patterson suit"! Mr. X's source, in turn, was "makeup sculptor Greg Smith, who had heard it from Burman himself."[26]

Once again, Chorvinsky proved nothing—but he did score a minor coup of sorts, being the first debunker to name Patterson's alleged Sasquatch stand-in. Alas, if subsequent revelations are true, he must be dead wrong.

While digging up "the goods" on Chambers—and adding a claim that Chambers built a "Burbank Bigfoot" replacement model for Frank Hansen's "Minnesota Iceman" after it was scrutinized by Ivan Sanderson and Bernard Heuvelmans in 1968—Chorvinsky explained his reason for never approaching Chambers directly. "I did not expect John Chambers to grant me an interview," Chorvinsky wrote, "so I conducted this investigation with the understanding that I would be tracking down rumors." Furthermore, he wrote "that it is important for investigators to think about rumors as they would any other information that they need to check out. Investigators, rather than shunning rumors, should go after them and try to determine if there is any basis for them in fact."[27]

In which case, we must rate his effort as a monumental failure. While choosing to reject the only first-hand testimony he received, from Tom Burman, Chorvinsky failed to substantiate any of the rumors linking Chambers to the Patterson film.

But he was not done trying, yet.

More than a year after his "exposé," in October 1997, Chorvinsky named director John Landis (*Animal House, The Blues Brothers, American Werewolf in London*, etc.) as another witness-once-removed to Chambers's participation in the Patterson film. More precisely, he cited Hollywood journalist Scott Essman, who quoted Landis's off-hand reference to "a makeup secret that only six people know"—i.e., that the "famous piece of eight-millimeter [*sic*] film of Bigfoot walking in the woods that was touted as the real thing was just a suit made by John Chambers."[28]

Among the several questions left unanswered: How did Landis learn the "secret"? And how did last year's "common knowledge" suddenly become a "secret that only six people know"? While seeming to challenge Landis, repeating his previous claim that "many makeup effects people have heard that Chambers made the suit and many believe that he did," Chorvinsky told his readers: "I have a call in to John Landis to see if he will elaborate on his remarks. The director is busy editing the sequel to *The Blues Brothers* and is currently hard to reach but I expect to hear from him or a representative shortly."[29]

Again, we must assume that he was disappointed. *Blues Brothers 2000* hit American theaters on 6 February 1998. Chorvinsky died from cancer on 16 July 2005, without releasing any further bulletins from Landis. In the meantime, however, Chambers himself had something to say.

On 26 October 1997—a week after the Landis "revelation" and six days past the Patterson film's thirtieth anniversary—Bigfoot researcher Bobbi Short interviewed John Chambers at the Motion Picture and Television Fund's retirement home in Woodland Hills, California. Seemingly unaware of the controversy Chorvinsky and others had generated surrounding his name, Chambers flatly denied either designing or manufacturing a Sasquatch costume for Roger Patterson. In the makeup man's own words, he was "good, but not that good."[30] Chambers died from complications of diabetes on 25 August 2001, at age seventy-eight.

Curiously, while never speaking directly to Chambers himself, Mark Chorvinsky had anticipated the news that shattered his pyramid of rumors. Chorvinsky's article from 1996 included a section titled "A Denial from Chambers," though in fact Chambers had made no statements at that time. His thesis—as with Tom Burman's denial of participation in a Bigfoot hoax—was a pre-emptive claim that any statement Chambers made would be a lie. Chorvinsky's "proof": a comment from Disney Studios makeup artist Bob Schiffer, who said, "I don't know if John [made the Patterson suit] but I'll tell you one thing—if he did he wouldn't tell you. It will die with him."[31]

In short, we are expected to swallow Chorvinsky's collection of unsubstantiated second- and third-hand gossip as "fact," while rejecting categorical denials from two alleged key players in the Patterson conspiracy—the "ape suit's" putative designer and his protégé, who supposedly wore it at Bluff Creek on 20 October 1967.

The mainstream media was happy to oblige. London's *Sunday Telegraph* trumpeted the Landis "exposé" on 19 October 1997, beneath a headline reading "Hollywood Admits to Bigfoot Hoax." E! Online—Web site for the same television network that has made global celebrities of Paris Hilton, the Kardashian clan, the Neiers sisters, and others famous simply for being famous—covered the "hoax" on 20 October 1997 with a new spurious twist, claiming that "Chambers, now 75, lives in a nursing home and is unable to confirm or deny the rumors."[32] In fact, as we have seen, he could and did deny the rumors, six days later.

Curiously, E! also pronounced Roger Patterson innocent of any part in the hoax. Howard Berger—who claimed only second-hand knowledge of the alleged fraud when interviewed by Mark Chorvinsky in 1996—now floated a bizarre new theory. "It was like a gag to be played on the guy who shot it," Berger said. "The guy never knew it was a hoax his friends played on him."[33]

Never? From 1967 to the moment of his death on 15 January 1972?

Clearly, if Berger is correct, all other theories branding Patterson a hoaxer must be false.

Confused and convoluted? Absolutely.

The last word on Patty? Not even close.

Unusual Suspects
Despite fatal flaws in the Chambers-Burman legend of 1996-97, it survives and still enjoys a certain currency today. Meanwhile, assorted other "experts" have suggested alternative theories and named different suspects as "Patty"—the apparent female Sasquatch depicted in Patterson's footage.

First up in the wake of the Chambers debacle was the British Broadcasting Corporation, tackling Sasquatch and other cryptids in six-part series called *The X Creatures*, airing on BBC 1 between 26 August and 30 September 1998. Patty's half-hour segment, broadcast on 16 September, was titled "Shooting Bigfoot."[34] It included a bumbling "recreation" of the Patterson film, employing an actor clad in an ape suit covered with long reddish hair, which bore no resemblance to Patty beyond the fact that both figures possessed one head and four limbs.

More important than BBC's shoddy special effects, however, was the network's handling of Bob Gimlin. The show's producers retrieved an interview Gimlin had granted in the early 1970s, then pared the lengthy transcript down to a single question. Asked whether the filming conceivably might have been hoaxed without his knowledge, Gimlin hesitated, then allowed that it was "possible," in theory. In 1998 the BBC's narrator closed "Shooting Bigfoot" with a flat—and false—assertion that Gimlin "now believes the film may be a hoax."[35] In fact, Gimlin said nothing of the kind. Months after *The X Creatures* episode aired, in January 1999, Gimlin told another interviewer, "I was there. I saw it. The film is genuine. Anybody who says different is just trying to make a buck."[36]

Next in line with an Sasquatch "exposé" was Rupert Murdoch's Fox Broadcasting Company, which aired a special program titled *World's Greatest Hoaxes: Secrets Finally Revealed* on 28 December 1998. Chosen as spokesman for the program's Bigfoot segment—and prepared to brand the Patterson film an "elaborate hoax"—was Kal K. Korff, a figure nearly as controversial as Sasquatch itself.[37]

Korff's profile on the *Skeptical Inquirer* Web site describes him as president and CEO of "TotalResearch, a company dedicated to studying universal mysteries and concerns," adding that he "is a former senior systems analyst at Lawrence Livermore National Laboratory on the 'Star Wars' program and is a recognized expert and pioneer in computer-based multimedia systems who helped develop Apple Computer's revolutionary HyperCard software—the ancestor to the Internet software Browser."[38]

Korff's own Web site, labeled CriticalThinkers.org, describes him in greater detail as "an internationally known, critically acclaimed Analyst, Author, Broadcaster, Columnist, Computer Systems Architect, Editor, Graphic Artist, Humanitarian Worker, Intelligence Analyst, Investigative Journalist, IT Specialist, Lecturer, Media Personality, Photo Editor, Senior Systems Analyst, Apple, Windows and Linux Software Developer, Teacher, WEB Architect, [and] Content Management System Designer. The President and CEO of CriticalThinkers.org, Kal is also a Counterterrorism Analyst, Advisor and Specialist, a Kidon Unit Commander [N.B.: The Israeli Mossad's covert assassination branch; *kidon* is "bayonet " in Hebrew] who fights against anti-Semitism and Islamofascist extremism. Kal holds the rank of Colonel in an Israeli-founded civilian entity. The author of nearly 50 non-fiction books, [and] over 10,000 articles, since 1975 Kal has lectured to more than 300,000 people worldwide."[39]

An impressive résumé, indeed—erroneous capitalization of common nouns notwithstanding—and one that is frequently challenged on various points by Korff's critics. While most of the claims are unverifiable, I note in passing that Korff's current *Skeptical Inquirer* profile lists him as the author of two books, not "nearly 50," and my searches online—at Book Finder, various branches of Amazon.com, etc.—raised the total to three. His own Web site, accessed on 13 July 2010 but no longer found online, revealed the same three titles and no more.[40] The same site's list of Korff-authored articles named two out of the rumored 10,000-plus.[41] He may indeed have published more; we simply cannot say.

Korff's online critics—ranging from reserved to rabid—accuse him of much more than mere puffery. In December 2006, one Paul Kimball wrote that "On his website, Korff claims, among many, many other things, to have been 'a key, expert witness in the O. J. Simpson murder trial CIVIL lawsuit.'"[42] [Emphasis in the original.] That claim did not appear on Korff's Web site in July 2010, but as Kimball demonstrates, it is—or would have been—blatantly false.

Another critic—this one carefully anonymous—allegedly researched Korff's claim of employment at California's Lawrence Livermore National Laboratory, verifying that Korff indeed worked there, while quoting several purported (unnamed) colleagues who deny Korff's link to "Star Wars" and relegate him to "remedial system support," while heaping on gratuitous insults.[43] How Mr. X obtained that information, if he did, remains a mystery.

Such wrangling is only pertinent in light of Korff's own mission statement for CriticalThinkers.org (now expunged from the Web). Online, he wrote:

> "As you can see from the content published here, which is updated dynamically [sic] as world events unfold, this Web site is dedicated to exposing the TRUTH about many diverse and sometimes controversial subjects, it presents some very hard facts.
>
> The greatest thing about facts, is that they ARE REALITY— anyone can independently verify them, should they wish to do so.
>
> The PROBLEM is, MOST people just don't bother to verify the information they either claim or "think" they know, for no valid nor logical reason. Since they don't do so, when REAL truth finally hits them, or they are forced to finally face facts, too often people resist it.
>
> People often get "upset" over what is REALLY REALITY, and in an act of denial some play the immoral game of "attack the messenger" while ignoring the message or the facts which are being communicated.
>
> Remember, just because one may not "like" certain facts, this does NOT give us the right to reject them.
>
> Facts, should NEVER be ignored—regardless of who states them, or what one "thinks" or feels about the person or source stating, sharing or proving them.

When listening to FACTS and considering them, logic should reign supreme, not emotions nor personal biases and desires.

Facts are INVIOLATE, they are (rightfully and thankfully) INDEPENDENT of anyone's "opinions."[44] [All emphasis in the original.]

We must keep those lofty principles in mind as we examine Korff's treatment of the Patterson film from 1998 onward. On *World's Greatest Hoaxes*, Korff told his audience, "There's no doubt in my mind that the Patterson film is a hoax. It is a human being in a fur suit." To name the culprit, Fox enlisted one Clyde Reinke, described as a rancher, businessman, and sometime "personal and administrative manager" of American National Enterprises—a film production/ distribution company based in Salt Lake City, Utah.[45]

In its day, ANE produced low-budget films that were long on stock footage and short on plot, including such forgettable features as *Mysteries from Beyond Earth* (1975) and *Are We Alone in the Universe?* (1978), both touting the probability of alien contact with humans. It also distributed the horror film *Piranha* in 1972.[46] One ANE participant—who described the firm as his "family's film business"—was Ronald Olson, a self-styled Sasquatch hunter who derived his inspiration from Roger Patterson. As Olson told a reporter in 1973, "I don't think I was even near the point of believing in it until I saw Patterson's footage. Not until I had seen the film and had worked with him for a while did I start coming to the point of thinking in my own mind that there was really something out there." Four years later, Olson wrote and produced his own crypto-mockumentary—*Sasquatch: The Legend of Bigfoot*—depicting the fictional adventures of seven intrepid monster hunters.[47]

But I digress.

On Fox, in December 1998, ANE manager Clyde Reinke identified Patterson's "man in the ape suit" as one Jerry Romney, an insurance agent formerly affiliated with the film company. Furthermore, Reinke claimed, Patterson himself had been a full-time salaried ANE employee, who faked the film at ANE's request and thereby made "millions" of dollars for the company. Fox interviewed Romney, who flatly contradicted Reinke and denied any role in the Patterson film. Stuck with that embarrassing development, Fox aired footage of Romney walking (in 1998), while narrator Lance Henrickson—himself the star of three Bigfoot horror films: *Sasquatch, Abominable,* and *Sasquatch Mountain*—remarked on the "similarity" between Romney's stride and Patty's, from 1967.[48]

Canadian researcher John Green set the story straight in 1999, declaring that Patterson had no affiliation with ANE until 1971, a few months before his death, when the firm bought limited rights to his footage for inclusion in future productions. "There is certainly a hoax involved here," said Green, "but not the one claimed by Fox. They are the ones who were hoaxed."[49]

Buckle Up
Round three in the Patterson-bashing marathon was frankly bizarre. In mid-January 1999,

working from computer enhancements of Patterson's footage prepared by Canadian researcher Christopher Murphy, Washington resident Cliff Crook proclaimed that he had found a metal buckle of some kind dangling from Patty's fur—proof positive that the film must be a hoax. "When the guy in the suit turned to look at the camera, it probably snapped loose and dangled from the fur," Crook said. "It's a hoax. Why would Bigfoot be wearing a belt buckle?"[50]

Why, indeed?

Crook's claim rated an article in the conservative news magazine *U.S. News & World Report*, whose editors were moved to chortle: "A shy and reclusive man-beast darts from a remote clearing in the Northern California woods and slips into the forest. But wait—what's that glittering at the creature's waist? A belt buckle? A bottle opener? Is it really Bigfoot, the legendary giant of the north woods, or just a guy in a monkey suit?"[51] *Skeptical Inquirer* also found the tale newsworthy, repeating it as late as spring 2002.[52]

Before evaluating his claim and its impact, it behooves us to take a closer look at Cliff Crook. Crook's Bigfoot Central Web site, online since 1980, proclaims him "America's first Bigfoot Case Investigator, starting with a May 1956 encounter that became the birth of the Bigfoot Case." Crook labels his Web site "North America's Official Bigfoot Case Database Headquarters," while adding the contradictory proviso that "We no longer extend Bigfoot report investigation services outside of Western Washington or beyond the perimeters of Klallam County." Finally, Crook claims that he inspired the character of Bigfoot researcher Wallace Wrightwood, portrayed by Don Ameche in the 1987 film *Harry and the Hendersons*. Beyond that, Crook says, he "was also technical advisor and sets supplier" for said movie.[53]

Concerning that film, Crook's claims are debatable. Critics suggest that Dr. Wrightwood was in fact a composite character, incorporating qualities borrowed from famed Bigfooters Peter Byrne, John Green, and Grover Krantz. As for Crook's role on the movie set, suffice it to say that his name appears nowhere in the exhaustive credits listed on the Internet Movie Database.[54]

Crook's problems do not end with film credits, however. Through the years, he has suffered storms of criticism—or "vicious lies," in his terms—from other members of the Sasquatch research community. Bigfoot Central declares that "99% of the malicious slanders posted against Cliff Crook and other long dedicated Bigfoot case investigators, is [*sic*] the work of one individual," whom he identifies as rival Matt Moneymaker, founder of the Bigfoot Field Researchers Organization.[55] And in fact, while some of the strongest criticism directed at Crook—for allegedly faking Bigfoot tracks, photos, etc.—does come from the BFRO, challenges to Crook's "discoveries" have also been voiced by Loren Coleman, Dr. Jeff Meldrum, and others.[56]

The strangest part of the "belt buckle" yarn is Christopher Murphy's involvement. According to online reporter Joseph Rose, "Murphy began questioning the film's validity after discovering an aberration in the footage while helping his son with a class project in 1995. Using a computer, he zoomed in tighter and tighter on the frames, finding what appears to be a glimmering ornate latch in the shape of a bottle opener." Murphy then allegedly told Rose that "there's something out of place" in the film, adding, "I have now sent my material to an expert in the [photo-enhancing] field."[57] Cliff Crook spoke for Murphy when he told *U.S. News & World Report*, "We think when the guy in the suit turned to look at the camera, it snapped loose and dangled from the fur."[58]

Whatever his qualms in January 1999, Murphy must have overcome them by July 2004, when he published *Meet the Sasquatch*, a collection of Bigfoot photographs analyzed in detail, sans any reference to dangling buckles. In April 2005 Murphy went on to publish *The Bigfoot Film Controversy*. The bulk of that volume—71 percent of its text—is a verbatim reprint of Roger Patterson's self-published book from 1966, *Do Abominable Snowmen of America Really Exist?* The remainder is a zealous defense of the Patterson film, with critiques of its detractors—except for Cliff Crook, who passes entirely unmentioned.[59]

The bottom line: most viewers of the film see nothing that resembles a buckle, bottle opener, or any other metallic object, regardless of enhancement or magnification. Crook continues to stand by his claim.

Long Time Coming
Before the ripples caused by Crook's "revelation" had time to subside, fresh conspiracy allegations surfaced at Zillah, in Washington's Yakima County. There, in January 1999, lawyer Barry Woodward announced that an unnamed client had dressed in Sasquatch-drag for Patterson's film. According to the *Yakima Herald-Republic*, "Woodward described the man only as a 58-year-old lifelong resident of the Yakima Valley who approached him a few months ago after a network news program called questioning authenticity of the 1967 film. The man wanted help negotiating a deal for rights to his story...as well as to explore any legal issues he might face as a result of his involvement in the hoax."[60]

Attorney Woodward also delivered a statement from a Yakima policeman, who subjected the anonymous ape impersonator to a polygraph examination and pronounced him truthful. Five days later, Woodward told the *Herald Republic*, "We're just sort of waiting for the dust to settle. We anticipate that we will be telling the full story to somebody rather quickly." In fact, another six years elapsed before the self-styled Patty-player spoke again and was identified at last. His story belongs to this chapter's final segment, but its fleeting debut is significant for the *Herald-Republic*'s first mention of one Greg Long, a Washington author and "paranormal researcher" engaged in writing a book on the Patterson film. Years in advance of final publication, Long branded Patterson a hoaxer. "It's all circumstantial evidence," he said. "But the circumstantial evidence is very convincing."[61]

While Long labored over his exposé, years in the making, yet another story surfaced to "prove" the Patterson footage a fraud. Notorious Sasquatch hoaxer Raymond Wallace died in Centralia, Washington, on 26 November 2002, and his family rushed to cash in on his passing, declaring him the inventor of Bigfoot and telling any reporter who'd listen that "Bigfoot just died."[62] The family sold film rights to his story for an undisclosed amount, to actor Judge Reinhold and his wife, but the movie was never produced.[63] Meanwhile, the story spun out of control and took on a life of its own.

In the initial version, son Michael Wallace told the *Seattle Times* that "his father called the Patterson film 'a fake' and said he had nothing to do with it. But he said his mother admitted she had been photographed in a Bigfoot suit." In the same article, Mark Chorvinsky—first to report the dubious claim that John Chambers made a Sasquatch suit for Patterson—declared that Michael Wallace "said his mother admitted she had been photographed in a Bigfoot suit."[64]

Two days later, the *Vancouver Sun* put a rather different twist on those claims, stating: "The most famous evidence for Bigfoot's existence, the so-called Patterson film...was another of Wallace's fakes, the family said—he told Patterson where to go to spot the creature and knew who had been inside the suit." Nephew David Wallace was quoted as telling the *Sun*, "He did it for the joke and then was afraid to tell anyone because they'd be so mad at him."[65]

Wallace's garbled story crossed the Atlantic on 7 December 2002, as *The Scotsman* told its readers: "Mr. Wallace later persuaded his wife to dress up in a monkey suit for 'Bigfoot' photographs, and he told Roger Patterson, a rodeo rider, to set up his camera to film the famous footage, shot in 1967, which supposedly showed the creature walking up the hillside."[66] On the same day, London's *Evening Telegram* reported that the Patterson film "was another of Mr. Wallace's fakes."[67]

By 2004 anthropologist David Daegling felt obliged to tell his readers that Ray Wallace "had a degree of involvement" in Patterson's film, which made the whole project suspect.[68] Four years later, Internet blogger Peter Ruble declared: "In a 1982 interview with a researcher, Wallace allegedly claimed that he acted as director of the Bigfoot film in Bluff Creak, CA. According to [Mark] Chorvinsky, "Wallace knew the identity of the man in the suit but insisted on taking it to his grave and would only say he was a Yakima American Indian."[69] The transcript of that interview remains as elusive as Sasquatch.

In fact, the only documented link between Roger Patterson and Ray Wallace was provided by Patterson himself, a full year before he caught Patty on film. His self-published book on Bigfoot mentions Wallace several times, in connection with the Sasquatch tracks found—or hoaxed—at Bluff Creek, California, in 1958. Sometime prior to the book's publication in 1966, Patterson visited Wallace at home in Toledo, Washington, where Wallace had settled in 1961. They discussed the Bluff Creek incident, and Patterson moved on. There is no reference to a second meeting, as claimed by Wikipedia's anonymous chronicler of the Patterson film. Any other claims of contact or collaboration between the two men is pure speculation.[70]

And in fact, for those who buy the previous hoax claims regarding John Chambers in Hollywood, the Wallace plot itself must be a fraud. The two accounts cannot be reconciled.

As of 2003, thirty-six years after Patty's film debut, five separate conspiracy theories had clashed and cancelled out one another, all without providing a shred of evidence that the footage was faked—by Patterson, or anyone else. A sixth "final solution" to the mystery was waiting in the wings, and as we'll see, it managed to present more contradictions than the other five combined.

Heironimus Botched

Thus far, between 1996 and 2002, critics of the Patterson film had named three different candidates for the role of "the man in the ape suit": Tom Burman, Jerry Romney, and Elna Wallace. Lawyer Barry Woodward added a fourth in February 1999, claiming that an anonymous client had contacted him "a few months ago after a network news program called, questioning the authenticity of the film."[71] That claim seems dubious today, since neither of the TV networks striving to debunk the Patterson film in 1998—BBC and Fox—identified Woodward's client as Patty. Fox placed its bet on Jerry Romney, who denied participation in the film, while BBC offered no candidates. Instead, we now know that the self-proclaimed Patty impersonator was approached for the first time by freelance author Greg Long, in early December 1998. Only then did the man contact Woodward.[72]

Who is Greg Long? His Northwest Mysteries Web site—the bulk of it still "under construction" in August 2010, missing from the Web entirely by April 2012—called him a "searcher for facts," a one-time English teacher, Peace Corps volunteer, and would-be novelist whose maiden literary effort never made it into print. Although committed to debunking Sasquatch, he proclaimed, "The world is a much stranger place than we think. There's something much bigger than Bigfoot out there. And it's real."[73]

As described in what Long calls his "monster of a book," his mission to discredit the Patterson film began on a barstool in 1995 and spanned the best part of a decade, climaxed with eventual publication in 2004. Long explains his crusade by saying that "The public deserves to hear the full, *factual* story of the Patterson film. I believe very strongly in this, so I have let the exact words of those who know the story speak for themselves....These people who knew the infamous Roger Patterson tell it like it was, as best they remember it....It is difficult to stand up in the midst of the herd and tell the truth as it is, because, in this case, it is an unpleasant, brutal truth. The public deserves it."[74] [Emphasis in the original.]

Kal Korff seconded that emotion in his foreword to Long's book. Having endorsed an entirely different Patty-player in 1998, Korff now cast his vote for Long's "historic milestone in the field of investigative journalism," praising Long as "truly a rare gem who stands out from among the many authors and interested parties nowadays who write about the so-called paranormal and profess to be 'investigators.' With Greg, you won't find any false claims, nor will you find supposition passed off or disguised as if it were fact."[75]

With that in mind, Long's readers must have been dismayed by his forays into amateur psychoanalysis and his repeated attempts to read the minds of individuals he never met. Regressing through time and to space Bluff Creek, California, on 20 October 1967, Long found Roger Patterson broadcasting "desperate fear" from his eyes, recalling dreams "he had fleshed out in the early hours of dawn," sensing "the big idea in the shadows," and so forth. "In his mind," Long surmised, "[Bigfoot] was silently moving through the trees alongside the road just ahead," and so on. All this, concerning the same mercenary hoaxer who (according to

Long) knows that Sasquatch doesn't exist, depicted in one fanciful scene, alone at his home, crowing to his mirror, "I'm goin' to make a million bucks!"[76]

Companion Bob Gimlin, meanwhile, is "apprehensive and vigilant," conscious that "Patterson was now submerged in thought, almost in a trance." Long tells us that "[c]old dread draped over Gimlin," aggravated when "a fetid odor suddenly filled the air."[77] Its source remains unclear, since—once again—Long has assured us that Sasquatch doesn't exist. Perhaps the costumed actor hired by Patterson had issues with personal hygiene?

Such baseless speculation and pseudo-psychology abounds throughout Long's text. Far from restricting it to distant sites in decades past, he also practiced on people whom he actually interrogated. Interviewee Jerry Merritt "projects a sense of dread," while Long intuits what another, Pat Mason, "must have thought...for years and years." Bob Gimlin, Long says, "apparently came under Patterson's spell." When Long's "man in the suit," Bob Heironimus, speaks, "a nervous twitch ripple[s] through his voice."[78] The list goes on and on.

Even then, Long's mind-reading pales beside his apparent malice toward some of his subjects. Roger Patterson bears much of the author's animus, habitually described as a "little man" who rides a "little," "small," or "puny" horse. Anonymous barroom witnesses brand Patterson a fraud and liar, thus launching Long's quest to expose him. Patterson manipulates, dupes or entrances all who cross his path—at least, when not cringing in dread from the stench of a monster that doesn't exist.[79]

Bob Gimlin fares little better with Long, emerging in print as a strange hybrid of gullibility and guile. "A hunched-over human form," when not under Patterson's "spell," Gimlin becomes "mysterious," "supposedly a horse breeder and cattleman," who winds up "bitter" and "discarded" by his larcenous partner in crime.[80]

And Long reserves a special venom for Bigfoot researchers who dispute his speculative theories. Canadian John Green—"tall, bony, and lugubrious"—"drones" interminably in a voice "edged with dreamy dullness," except when he "fumes" in response to Long's prodding. René Dahinden "raves" in an accent that Long can't resist mocking—"I vas clueless"; "I vouldn't do that!"—*ad nauseam*. His excuse, dished up in advance, is a pretense of objectivity: "I retain throughout the book the local dialect, inflection, and syntax of the witnesses wherever possible."[81]

Or, at least, wherever it makes them sound foolish.

How does Long fare when dealing with objective facts? Should we begin with his description of Patty's "pinkish soles," in fact a shade of gray on every color print of the Patterson footage? [82] Or is it best to move directly to his contradictory descriptions of the Patterson "ape suit"?

Bob Heironimus initially told Long that Patterson's suit was a three-piece affair. The "head" was something "like an old-time football helmet" with a mask attached. Heironimus "sensed that the mask was made of leather, but he wasn't sure." Below the helmet was "a corset or middle piece between the neck and waist," fashioned from the malodorous hide of "a dead, red horse" that Patterson had killed and flayed. Heironimus could not describe the sleeves, but recalled that the costume's hands "felt like stiff leather gloves." Patty's artificial breasts were "solid," not "bouncy." As to their means of attachment, Heironimus "never gave it much thought." The costume's "legs" consisted of rubber hip boots with the feet cut off, replaced by "old house slippers you used to see around, that looked like a big foot with toes on them." Over everything, Patterson had "attached or glued fur from an old fur coat." Although Heironimus was never fitted for the suit, he managed to wear it over his street clothes.[83]

If that getup sounds little or nothing like Patty on film, we should not be dismayed. Heironimus also claimed that on the day of the filming, he performed for Patterson's camera at Willow Creek, some twenty miles southwest of the actual Bluff Creek film site. That gaffe prompts Long to wonder if Heironimus is lying, but he finally decides to let it slide without resolving the discrepancy.[84]

The strange description of Patterson's homemade ape suit becomes more significant in Long's last chapter, when he scores a "breakthrough" with discovery of North Carolina costume-maker Phil Morris. In November 2003, with Long's manuscript ostensibly finished, Morris claimed that he had sold a gorilla suit to Patterson in August 1967. The suit consisted of six pieces—the main body with four limbs, plus detachable head, hands, and feet—all made from knitted cloth with thousands of artificial hairs sewn on by a machine. In short, it bore no resemblance whatever to the suit described by Heironimus—and, as amply indicated by published photographs, it likewise looked nothing like Patty.[85]

What's a truth-seeker to do with such glaring contradictions? Morris did his best to help Long, describing a follow-up phone call from Patterson, wherein Morris coached him on how to flesh out Patty's shoulders (football pads) and extend the arms (by inserting sticks). Heironimus recalled no such features—and plainly described his hands sliding into leather gloves—but Long charged merrily ahead. The Morris ape mask is also wildly different from Patty's face on film, but Morris helpfully suggests that "maybe Patterson brought in somebody to work on the face." He fantasizes Patterson building a facial mold from plaster of Paris, creating a lifelike rubber mask to suit his needs, and so on. And Patty's breasts? Long speculates that "Patterson could have attached black balloons filled with sand to the front of the suit." All that's missing is a single shred of evidence. Ignoring all discrepancies—and his primary informant's published statements—Long concluded that "Heironimus had simply worn the suit and walked in it, and hadn't examined it."[86]

Luckily for all concerned, the suit is missing. Heironimus claims that Patterson and Gimlin ordered him to stash it in the trunk of his car, from which it later disappeared. In another flight of fantasy, Long tells us: "Later, at night, Patterson and Gimlin, unseen, removed the suit from the trunk." According to whom? Perhaps Patterson's ghost. Indeed, Long describes himself lying in bed and beaming telepathic questions to the late Bigfoot-hunter: "'Roger,' I thought, 'Roger, what are you going to do? What are you going to do? Bob's breaking the silence.'"[87]

Before ending his narrative, Long finds time to praise foreword-author Kal Korff for "upset

[ting] the Bigfoot community" in December 1998, with his performance on Fox's *World's Greatest Hoaxes*. Carefully excised is Jerry Romney, named in that broadcast as the "man in the ape suit." If that glaring omission agitated Korff, flying in the face of his stated belief that "Facts, should NEVER be ignored," he lodged no public protest.[88]

He Said/She Said

Early reviews of Long's book, collected by his publisher and echoed verbatim by conspiracy theorist Jeff Rense, were predictably ecstatic. Robert Kiviat, producer of the 1998 Fox special that triggered denials from Jerry Romney, scuttled his own production to praise Long's "highly informative and revealing investigation." Debunker Kenneth Wylie—armed with a Ph.D. in African studies, whose 1980 volume *Bigfoot: A Personal Inquiry into a Phenomenon* restricts its focus to the author's home state of Michigan—found Long's tome both "a very good read" and "a serious book that reveals an 'actual' conspiracy of deliberate lies." Anthropologist Dawn Prince-Hughes deemed *The Making of Bigfoot* "a rare book: one that celebrates the true mysteries of our lives while remaining faithful to the importance of rigorous examination and critical thinking." Michaela Kocis—a Czech radio broadcaster, described in *Skeptical Inquirer* as "the first journalist to write a definitive exposé article series on Greg Long's research, having been given exclusive access to the investigative team"—opined that Long's book "should set an example for courses on critical thinking and investigative journalism around the world."[89]

In fact, the only "team" in evidence—discounting Long's wife, who served as his photographer and sounding board—consisted of Kocis herself, with Kal Korff. Four months after *The Making of Bigfoot* hit bookshelves, they joined forces to plug the book via an article in the July/August issue *Skeptical Inquirer*. That piece referred to Korff's foray on Fox—"it caused a sensation"—and repeated Clyde Reinke's discredited claim that Roger Patterson helped American National Enterprises "cook up" the Bluff Creek film. And once again, Korff failed to mention Fox's (and his own) endorsement of Jerry Romney as Patty. Instead, Korff said the Fox broadcast caused Heironimus to confess.[90]

Moving on, Korff and Kocis claimed that Opal Heironimus—Bob's mother—saw and remembered Patterson and Gimlin returning a horse to her barn, prior to removing their Bigfoot costume from the trunk of Bob's car. Strangely, Long had previously told his readers that both events—the return and the theft—occurred "unnoticed" and "unseen."[91]

The most startling—some might say hilarious—part of the *S.I.* article appeared under a subheading called "The Eye Has It." There, Korff claimed a personal discovery from enlarged frames of the Bluff Creek film. Patty's right eye, he said, displays "a sudden burst of light...which cannot be explained by normal sunlight reflecting off an organic eye." Korff's conclusion: the gleam is a pointer to a glass eye worn by Bob Heironimus! Alas, in his description of the hairy "football helmet" with a mask dangling an inch or more in front of his face, Heironimus told Long, "I couldn't see out real good because my eyes were set back from the eye holes."[92]

Unfazed by such glaring—or gleaming?—contradictions, Korff and Kocis finished strong, declaring that "Since the publication of Long's book, the media reaction has been overwhelmingly positive. The mainstream press is no longer taking the Patterson Bigfoot film seriously as evidence of anything but a hoax."[93] It's tempting to ask when the "mainstream press" ever *had* accepted the film as evidence of Bigfoot's existence, but the odds of a serious answer are nil.

Friends of Roger Patterson and serious Bigfoot researchers soon replied to Long and Korff. Florence Merritt Showman, a relative of Long's dread-filled witness Jerry Merritt, penned a letter to the *Yakima Herald-Republic*, flatly declaring that her family's home "never at any time was a Bigfoot headquarters as Long wrote in his book," and that "the Merritts had no involvement in the Patterson and Gimlin Bigfoot film."[94]

Sasquatch researcher Daniel Perez, writing to *Fortean Times*, dissected Long's work in detail, beginning with the flyleaf's spurious claim that Patterson's film "has managed to fool scores of scientists." He noted Korff's and Long's clumsy evasion of the Jerry Romney gaffe from 1998, suggesting that Long and Robert Kiviat collaborate on a new TV special titled "Secrets Revealed: How We Substituted Romney For Heironimus And Duped The American Public!"[95]

Loren Coleman, reviewing Long's book for *Fate* magazine, called it "a well-orchestrated character assassination of Roger Patterson....At 475 pages, it is badly in need of more editing and less about when Greg Long eats chocolate doughnuts (p. 354). Two-thirds of this book is mostly flowery prose that you will have to endure to locate the kernel of the story. That core turns out to be a 'he said/he said' tale viewed through Greg Long's biased sunglasses."[96]

From Russia, veteran yeti researchers Dmitri Bayanov and Igor Bourtsev joined the chorus, declaring that "By failing to re-create the alleged Bigfoot costume and re-enact the film Kal Korff and Greg Long have exposed themselves as sham investigators and presumptuous men."[97]

John Green also weighed in from Canada, ignoring Long's personal insults while detailing errors from the book and the Korff-Kocis article in a letter to *Skeptical Inquirer*. Happily, for his targets, Green's rebuttal exceeded the magazine's maximum word-count for letters, and thus went unpublished. If it had run, *S.I.* readers would have learned that Patterson had no relationship with ANE prior to the Bluff Creek filming; that the dead-horse suit described by Bob Heironimus bore no resemblance to any made by Philip Morris; that Heironimus contradicted himself on details of his role in the filming, first claiming in print that Bob Gimlin approached him, later telling TV reporters that Patterson made the first overture; that Korff falsely dated the first Heironimus "confession" from 2003, ignoring his revelations to lawyer Barry Woodward five years earlier; and that the mainstream media's reaction to Long's book, far from being a landslide of acclaim, was "pretty much non-existent."[98]

In parting, Green proposed that "For the sake of its own reputation *The Skeptical Enquirer* [*sic*] should ask its associated organization, the Council for Media Integrity, to take a truly skeptical look at the piece of puffery the *Enquirer* [*sic*] has recently published promoting Greg Long's *The Making of Bigfoot*."[99] No such self-examination was forthcoming.

Barking Mad

When Korff and Long replied to their critics, they seemed to speak with a single voice—or, at least, to adopt the same frantic style. Korff's now-defunct Web site displayed a strange fondness for random capitalization, generally viewed on the Web as intemperate shouting. In the heat of battle, Long mimicked his cheerleader's style—and, in some cases, his very words.

Korff led off on 8 March 2004—one week after his joint appearance with Long, Kiviat and Kocis on Jeff Rense's radio show—with a posting to the Rense Web site. After declaring that "radio history was made" during the first broadcast, he crowed, "For the first time EVER, you were TOLD THE TRUTH about how the infamous Roger Patterson hoax 1967 'Bigfoot' film was made." He aimed another pitch at potential buyers—"The book is brand new, in great demand, and can be purchased for less than $20.00. This is a small price to 'pay' for the truth."—but somehow, Korff got confused. The cover price listed by Prometheus Books, then as now, was $25.98. Having delivered the plug, Korff turned on his detractors in familiar ungrammatical style.

> Notice this truth did NOT come from the "Bigfoot community"—which really does not exist in any tangible sense...There are several members of this self-proclaimed "community" that are now very upset. Their reactions are very emotional, and one important FACT must NOT be forgotten: NONE of them can PROVE that the man WE CLAIM wore the Bigfoot suit, IS WRONG or not telling the truth! They CANNOT prove that the man we are now offering to the public, is lying....Tonight, our Bigfoot Investigation Team [*sic*], especially myself, expect to be attacked on the Jeff Rense Program. We will be attacked emotionally, and according to the rumors, We [*sic*] have to LAUGH at this notion. Do you think gravity CARES if people do not want to believe that it exists? Do you think the rain CARES of people think [*sic*] it is "horrible" that it is raining out? NO, they do not, and they SHOULD not. Our "critics" sometimes mean well, but are fundamentally MISGUIDED. They have FORGOTTEN ONE RULE OF SCIENCE AND EVIDENCE: that extraordinary claims, require extraordinary proof. WE HAVE SUPPLIED OUR BEST EVIDENCE, IT IS IN THE FORM OF GREG LONG'S BRUISING, AND DEFINITIVE EXPOSE OF THE ROGER PATTERSON "BIGFOOT" FILM HOAX. Our "critics" will do EVERYTHING BUT DISPROVE US, BECAUSE THEY CANNOT. So when they start attacking us, especially me, with emotional claims that I am a "debunker" or a "skeptic"—I will NOT let such reckless charges stand. They are FALSE and they are LIES, and those making such claims WILL be held ACCOUNTABLE and EXPOSED....As you listen to their "case"...ask yourselves these three questions: 1) Are they calling us debunkers or skeptics? IF so,

they are LYING, there is nothing further to discuss. 2) HAVE THEY PROVEN that Bob Heironimus is NOT the man who wore the Bigfoot suit? The ANSWER IS NO! 3) Have they PROVEN Phillip Morris did NOT make the Bigfoot suit that he sold to Roger Patterson? The answer once AGAIN, is NO!! Until they DISPROVE AND ADDRESS THESE THREE ISSUES, THERE IS NOTHING FURTHER TO DISCUSS. THEY CAN COMPLAIN, BUT THAT IS ALL....OUR EXPOSE IS JUST BEGINNING. I CALL ON, AND CHALLENGE, MR. BOB GIMLIN TO CONFESS THE HOAX, TO FINALLY TELL THE TRUTH. MR.GIMLIN, FEEL FREE TO SUE US IN COURT FOR LIBEL AND SLANDER. JUST REMEMBER THAT THESE CHARGES GO BOTH WAYS....Mr. Gimlin, YOU, sir, so far, can't seem to pass the "smell" or "credibility test". WE WILL NOT REST UNTIL YOU ARE BROUGHT TO JUSTICE, AND YOU CONFESS THE TRUTH ABOUT YOUR INVOLVEMENT IN THE PATTERSON BIGFOOT HOAX, which you CONTINUE to deceive people on, and make money on, by selling to consumers, a story that is NOT true, and because it is NOT true, you are leading people to BUY what they BELIEVE is true, but it IS NOT. That is CONSUMER FRAUD, AND WE WILL NOW COOPERATE WITH AUTHORITIES TO PROVIDE EVIDENCE FOR PROSECUTION UNDER THE CONSUMER FRAUD STATUTES. If ANYONE in the Bigfoot "community" has a "problem" with trying to hold Mr. Gimlin ACCOUNTABLE for his role in the Patterson HOAX, then it is because the Bigfoot "community" has a PROBLEM WITH THE TRUTH.[100]

Having declared himself a force of nature, on a par with gravity and rain, Korff's final salvo was bizarre. Long's book, if it can be believed, made the case that *no one* earned a profit from the Bluff Creek film except, Long claims, for Patterson himself and his mythical partners at ANE.

Long himself backed Korff's broadside with a message of his own on Rense.com, praising Korff even as he seemed to hold Kal at arm's length. He led with a statement that "Kal Korff has written the introduction to *The Making of Bigfoot*, but nothing else in my book, except a few paragraphs that I edited that form his account of solving the 'feet' problem on the Bigfoot. That particular item about the Bigfoot's fake feet are [*sic*] dealt with in my book. Kal has reviewed my facts, as has Kiviat, and that's it. So, I'm totally independent of these two gentlemen as far as my findings go."[101] In fact, as author Long should know, he wrote the introduction to his own book. Korff supplied a short *foreword*, clearly identified as such.[102]

After that muddled start, Long turned to an obligatory defense of his ally, channeling Korff in the process. "Also," he wrote, "this fiction that Korff is a 'debunker' is another falsehood. My Webster's New World College Dictionary defines the word 'debunk' this way: 'to expose the false or exaggerated claims of' something. Well, that's what I do in my book, I expose a false claim. And that's what Kal is doing. But he's NOT A DEBUNKER IN THE SENSE of A

CLOSE-MINDED SKEPTIC. I know Kal's working on many other projects where the truth must be told. One is terrorism; he's working on a book called Secret Wars; and I've got a glimpse of it. Believe me, people are going to be wildly surprised by that book."[103]

The surprise, in fact, will occur if that book is ever published. Initially advertised on Amazon.com as a February 2004 hardcover release, *Secret Wars* has yet to appear in print. Eight years later, its Amazon page still urges customers to "Sign up to be notified when this item becomes available." As of April 2012, an anonymous review states that the supposed publisher, Prometheus Books, "has publicly stated that they WILL NOT be publishing this book, ever."[104]

In closing, Long awkwardly paraphrased Korff:

> "Finally, I want to say that Bob Kiviatt [*sic*] and Kal Korff are COMMITTED AND DEDICATED TO FINDING THE TRUTH. I've never met in my life two of the hardest working individuals in the fields of television documentary and the print media than these two guys [*sic*]. NEVER. I know for a fact that their main goal is to GET TO THE BOTTOM OF CONTROVERSIAL AND DEBATED CASES AND TO PRESENT EVIDENCE THAT MIGHT POINT TO OR PROVE A REAL, UNEXPLAINED PHENOMENON EXISTS. Every word I've written in The Making of Bigfoot has been published on strict standards of EVIDENCE and WHAT WOULD STAND UP IN A COURT OF LAW. [N.B.: Presuming unsupported hearsay were admissible, which it is not.] My findings are BEYOND A REASONABLE DOUBT. I've been asked tough questions by Kal and Bob Kiviatt [*sic*]; believe me, they haven't left me off the hook [*sic*]. Their role in the whole Patterson affair is to get the truth out to the world. It's as simple as that. The public has the right to know. It's time for flim-flam and unbased [*sic*], unsupported claims to END. I welcome people who can PROVE ME WRONG in The Making of Bigfoot. I know I'm NOT WRONG, but if people feel otherwise, they NEED TO DISPROVE ME [*sic*]."[105]

In other venues, Korff pursued his empty threats to jail Bob Gimlin for a nonexistent crime. In an email to John Green, he wrote: "As for ME, I WANT to see Gimlin PROSECUTED and am WORKING TO ACHIEVE THIS. I just hope he does not run and 'confess' to Kiviat before my work with the Attorney General is complete. If Gimlin 'comes clean' to Kiviat before I finish, he probably WON'T be prosecuted. I hope he DOES get nailed, because consumer fraud IS CONSUMER FRAUD. I also expect to fly out (unless I can accomplish the same from over here) to give a deposition to the Attorney General's office for CONSUMER FRAUD...specifically Gimlin's comments over Sasquatch: Legend Meets Science."[106] Most readers of this article will recognize Korff's allusion to a documentary special broadcast by the Discovery Channel on 9 January 2003—from which Bob Gimlin earned precisely nothing.

Greg Long, meanwhile, reserved his harshest prose for Dmitri Bayanov, delivered in a May 2004 email. Long wrote:

> Dmitri, Here's what it comes down to: you, like every other ignorant Patterson film worshiper, embrace an UTTER LIE fabricated and executed by a CON MAN, an UNEMPLOYED BUM who purposely wouldn't work for a living and who chose to CHEAT AND LIE AND STEAL to make his way through his short life. By the way, JOHN GREEN is TOTALLY MISINFORMED when he says Patterson was an HONEST MAN. Maybe JOHN GREEN should get off his ass and go talk to VILMA RADFORD, who Patterson RIPPED OFF. It is your job to DISPROVE EVERY STATEMENT OF EVERY PERSON IN MY BOOK, a book which I guarantee you have NOT READ. You know why you have not read it: you are a CLOSED-MINDED FOOL. I've watched BOB HEIRONIMUS walk and he walks like the Bigfoot in the Patterson HOAX FILM. Same arm swing, same cupped hands, same bowed shoulders, same gait. [N.B. The same argument used in 1998 to identify "man in the suit" Jerry Romney.] ...You are a VERY STUPID man to declare that he is a liar without even meeting him, without performing character checks, and without digging into his background. The same goes for everyone else being copied on this email....By the way, regarding this idiotic "IM" or BODY INDEX, what the hell does it even mean? ... Get off this STUPID IM crap. Regarding the BIGFOOT TRACKS, they were FAKED after the filming. Prove they weren't!!! Regarding this VERITABLE PILE OF GARBAGE relating to SCARS ON THE WRIST, TUMORS, HERNIAS, SUPPURATING EYE: all crimps in the suit and optical artifacts detected by the FILM WORSHIPER AS THY [sic] STUDY DEEPER AND DEEPER THE "MYSTERIES" OF THE FILM IMAGES....PHILIP MORRIS manufactured the GORILLA SUIT that Patterson used. Go contact him, Dimitri [sic]. AGAIN, YOU NEVER READ THE BOOK. By the way, why didn't JEFF MELDRUM get off his ASS when he entered the Bigfoot field and do the proper "on the ground" investigation of Roger Patterson and all the players over in Yakima like any good scientiss [sic] would. MELDRUM doesn't believe that CON ARTISTS exist, or PATHOLOGICAL LIARS. He is too far GONE deep within his academic studies over in Idaho and too much of a BLIND BELIEVER IN THE HOAX FILM to get out of it now. If he's the best SCIENTIST you can trot out to talk about the Patterson film, your group is in DEEP DOO-DOO. I notice that he is LYING LOW these days, VERY LOW. Why is that? I think he's work [sic] on a COSTUME BOOK, or something dealing with MORMON HISTORY AND GENETICS,

MAYBE TO PROVE BIGFOOT IS REALLY A DISPLACED AFRICAN APE THAT SOMEHOW GOT OVER HERE WITH ELEPHANTS AND TIGERS WHEN THE ANCIENT HEBREWS POPPED UP IN NORTH AMERICA IN JOSEPH SMITH'S FAKE HISTORY BOOK? I've got to go, Dimitri [*sic*]. Let me know when you actually READ MY BOOK. By the way, how do you know that the Patterson film isn't REPRODUCIBLE? Haven't you tried it? Greg Long (my father's name: Boris Danielovitch Suslov)[107]

Long's confusion over "this STUPID IM crap" is sadly typical. The intramembral (IM) index, discovered by German-born anthropologist Adolf Hans Schultz (1891-1976), is a ratio used to compare limb proportions, expressed as a percentage, frequently in primatology since it helps predict primate locomotor patterns. It is equal to the length of forelimbs (humerus plus radius) divided by the length of the hind limbs (femur plus tibia) multiplied by 100. For scores lower than 100, the forelimbs are shorter than the hind limbs, as is common in leaping primates and bipedal hominids. Quadrupedal primates tend to have scores around 100, while brachiating primates (those that swing from tree limbs by their arms) have scores significantly higher than 100. The formula has been recognized worldwide since 1937—except, apparently, by Greg Long.

Whatever Long and his "Bigfoot Investigation Team" believe they have proved, amidst all of his book's contradictions, supposition, and hearsay—buttressed by their hysterical attacks on those with the temerity to disagree—one thing is crystal-clear. Somewhere between the launching of their search in 1998 and their furious emails in 2004, they lost sight of Korff's maxim that "When listening to FACTS and considering them, logic should reign supreme, not emotions nor personal biases and desires." Clearly, based on their *ad hominem* attacks and empty threats of prosecution for nonexistent crimes, they had lapsed into what Korff calls "the immoral game of 'attack the messenger.'"[108]

Sound and fury, signifying nothing.

Nine years on and counting, the Korff-Long "investigation" that was "just beginning" has produced no further revelations. No one has been "held accountable and exposed" for calling Korff and Long debunkers—which, by Long's own public admission, they are. No prosecutor anywhere has charged Bob Gimlin with a crime. Both "truth-seekers" have removed their Web sites from the Internet. Despite Korff's boast that Long's tome "HAS ALREADY BECOME the BESTSELLING, AND THE FASTEST SELLING BOOK ON BIGFOOT OF ALL TIME," it stands eclipsed by works from Jeff Meldrum, Loren Coleman, John Green, and the late Ivan Sanderson.[109]

And the rest, we may hope, is silence.

References

1.   Grover Krantz, *Bigfoot Sasquatch Evidence* (Blaine, WA: Hancock House, 1999), pp. 87-124.
2.   Jeff Meldrum, *Sasquatch: Legend Meets Science* (New York: Tom Doherty, 2006), pp. 137-78.
3.   Daniel Perez, "The Patterson Film: A Discussion," *Bigfoot Encounters*, http://www.bigfootencounters.com/articles/forteantimes05.htm.
4.   David Daegling, *Bigfoot Exposed: An Anthropologist Examines America's Enduring Legend* (Lanham, MD: AltaMira Press, 2004), p. 112.
5.   Krantz, op cit.; Meldrum, op cit.
6.   Mark Chorvinsky, "Some Thoughts About the Patterson Bigfoot Film on its 30th Anniversary," *Strange Magazine* (October 1997), http://www.strangemag.com/pattersonfilm30th.html.
7.   John Napier, *Bigfoot: The Sasquatch and Yeti in Myth and Reality* (New York: E. P. Dutton, 1973) pp. 89, 95.
8.   Don Hunter and René Dahinden, *Sasquatch/Bigfoot: The Search for North America's Incredible Creature* (Richmond Hill, Ontario: Firefly Books, 1993), p. 119.
9.   Greg Long, *The Making of Bigfoot* (Amherst, NY: Prometheus, 2004), p. 188.
10.   Krantz, p. 120.
11.   Daegling,, p. 119.
12.   Bob Young, "Lovable trickster created a monster with Bigfoot hoax," *Seattle Times*, December 5, 2002.
13.   "John Chambers," IMDB, http://www.imdb.com/name/nm0150357.
14.   Mark Chorvinsky, "The Makeup Man and the Monster," *Strange Magazine* 17 (Summer, 1996), http://www.strangemag.com/chambers17.html.
15.   Chorvinsky; "John Chambers," IMDB.
16.   Chorvinsky.
17.   "Donald F. Glut," IMDB, http://www.imdb.com/name/nm0323304.
18.   Chorvinsky.
19.   Ibid.
20.   Ibid
21.   Ibid.
22.   Ibid.; "Bob Burns," IMDB, http://www.imdb.com/name/nm0122591.
23.   Chorvinsky; "Bart Mixon," IMDB, http://www.imdb.com/name/nm0122591; "Jim McPherson," IMDB, http://www.imdb.com/name/nm0574237.
24.   Chorvinsky.
25.   Ibid.
26.   Ibid.
27.   Ibid.
28.   Mark Chorvinsky, "Update: Film Director John Landis Goes Public Concerning Makeup Master John Chambers' Involvement In The Famous Patterson Bigfoot Film," *The Strange Report*, http://www.strangemag.com/landischambers.html.
29.   Ibid.

30. Loren Coleman, "John Chambers Denies Involvement in Patterson Bigfoot Film," Bigfoot Encounters, http://www.bigfootencounters.com/hoaxes/loren.htm.

31. Chorvinsky, "The Makeup Man and the Monster."

32. Ken Neville, "Bigfoot Movie: A Hollywood Hoax? " E! Online, http://www.eonline.com/news/Bigfoot_Movie__A_Hollywood_Hoax_/35365.

33. Ibid.

34. "The X Creatures," http://en.wikipedia.org/wiki/The_X_Creatures.

35. "Shooting Bigfoot," *The X Creatures*, BBC 1, 16 September 1998.

36. Loren Coleman, *Bigfoot!* (New York: Paraview, 2003), p. 106.

37. Ibid., p. 101.

38. "Kal K. Korff, " Skeptical Inquirer, http://www.csicop.org/author/kalkkorff.

39. WHO and WHAT is Kal Korff?" http://www.kalkorff.com/index.php?option=com_content&view=article&id=52&Itemid=88.

40. "Kal Korff's Books-Videos," http://www.kalkorff.com/index.php?option=com_wrapper&view=wrapper&Itemid=82.

41. "Kal Korff's Articles," http://www.kalkorff.com/index.php?option=com_content&view=category&layout=blog&id=70&Itemid=81.

42. Paul Kimball, "Kal Korff and Glass Houses," The Other Side of Truth, http://redstarfilms.blogspot.com/2006/12/kal-korff-and-glass-houses.html.

43. "Kal Did Work At LLNL," Kult of Kal Korff, http://kultofkal.blogspot.com/2009/03/kal-did-work-at-llnl.html.

44. "About Us," CriticalThinkers.org, http://www.kalkorff.com.

45. he Patterson Film: A Discussion by Daniel Perez,"Bigfoot Encounters, http://www.bigfootencounters.com/articles/forteantimes05.htm.

46. "American National Enterprises," IMDB, http://www.imdb.com/company/co0080674.

47. Doug Bates, "The man who chases Bigfoot," *The Register-Guard* (Eugene, OR), October 21, 1973; "Ronald D. Olson," IMDB, http://www.imdb.com/name/nm2309390.

48. Coleman, pp. 102-3; "The Patterson Film: A Discussion by Daniel Perez."

49. Coleman, p. 104.

50. Joseph Rose, "Sasquatch: Man in a Monkey Suit?" Wired News (19 January 1999), http://www.wired.com/culture/lifestyle/news/1999/01/17398.

51. Lynn Rosellini, "Not so big after all," *U.S. News & World Report* 126 (25 January 1999): 61.

52. Ben Radford, "Bigfoot at 50," Skeptical Inquirer 26 (March/April 2002), http://www.csicop.org/si/show/bigfoot_at_50_evaluating_a_half-century_of_bigfoot_evidence.

53. Bigfoot Central, http://www.angelfire.com/biz/bigfootcentral and http://www.angelfire.com/biz/bigfootcentral/cliff.html.

54. "Harry and the Hendersons," IMDB, http://www.imdb.com/title/tt0093148/trivia and http://www.imdb.com/title/tt0093148/fullcredits#cast.

55. Bigfoot Central, http://www.angelfire.com/biz/bigfootcentral and http://www.angelfire.com/biz/bigfootcentral/moneymakers.html.

56. Matt Moneymaker, "Hoaxer Cliff Crook promoting Phony Photo, again," BFRO (30 January 2010), http://www.bfro.net/REF/hoax.asp; Loren Coleman, "First Bigfoot Investigator Was Crook?" Cryptomundo (27 January 2010), http://www.cryptomundo.com/cryptozoo-news/crook2010; Mike Archbold, "'America's first Bigfoot investigator' finds

new footprints," *The News Tribune* (Tacoma, WA), 27 January 2010.

57. Rose.

58. Rosellini.

59. Christopher Murphy, *Meet the Sasquatch* (Blaine, WA: Hancock House, 2004); Roger Patterson and Christopher Murphy, *The Bigfoot Film Controversy* (Blaine, WA: Hancock House, 2005).

60. David Wasson, "Bigfoot unzipped--man claims it was him in a suit." Herald-Republic (*Yakima*, WA) 30 January 1999.

61. David Wasson, "Bigfoot believers say film no hoax," *Herald-Republic*, 4 February 1999.

62. Bob Young, "Lovable trickster created a monster with Bigfoot hoax," *Seattle Times*, 5 December 2002.

63. "Wallace Scam Ensnares Hollywood Producers," BFRO, http://www.bfro.net/news/Wallace.asp#producers.

64. Young.

65. "Footprints big but 42-year Bigfoot hoax even larger," *Vancouver Sun*, 7 December 2002.

66. Quoted by Loren Coleman, "How Wallace Was Blamed For the Patterson Bigfoot Film," Cryptomundo, http://www.cryptomundo.com/cryptozoo-news/elna-as-bf.

67. Oliver Poole, "That's not Bigfoot, that's my wife," *Evening Telegram*, 7 December 2002.

68. David Daegling, *Bigfoot Exposed: An Anthropologist Examines America's Enduring Legend* (Lanham, MD: Altamira Press, 2004), p. 117.

69. "The Bigfoot Hoax—Was Ray Wallace of Tacoma the Official Mastermind?" http://voices.yahoo.com/the-bigfoot-hoax-was-ray-wallace-tacoma-official-1858412.html?cat=38

70. Patterson, *Do Abominable Snowmen of America Really Exist?*, p. 73; "Patterson-Gimlin film," Wikipedia, http://en.wikipedia.org/wiki/Patterson-Gimlin_film.

71. Wasson.

72. Linda Ashton, "Man Claims to be Bigfoot in Famous 1967 Sasquatch Film," *The Oregonian* (Portland, OR), 2 February 1999.

73. "About Greg Long," Northwest Mysteries, http://northwestmysteries.com/aboutgreglong/default.htm.

74. Greg Long, *The Making of Bigfoot* (Amherst, NY: Prometheus, 2004), pp. 14-15, 29.

75. Kal Korff, foreword to *The Making of Bigfoot*, pp. 9-11.

76. Long, pp. 19-27.

77. Ibid.

78. Ibid., pp. 115, 140, 146, 159.

79. Ibid., pp. 19-27, 30-1, 159, etc.

80. Ibid., pp. 152, 157, 159, 161, etc.

81. Ibid., pp. 178-80, 182-3, 190-3, etc.

82. Ibid., p. 22.

83. 83. Ibid., pp. 344-6, 355.

84. Ibid., p. 348.

85. Ibid., pp. 446, 449, 460.

86. Ibid., pp. 355, 447-8, 453, 458.

87. Ibid., pp. 350-1, 358.

88. Ibid., pp. 451-2; Kal Korff, CriticalThinkers.org, http://www.kalkorff.com.

89. Long, flyleaf and back cover; Rense.com, http://www.rense.com/general49/making.htm;

Kal Korff and Michaela Kocis, "Exposing Roger Patterson's 1967 Bigfoot film hoax," Skeptical Inquirer (July/August 2004), http://www.bigfootencounters.com/articles/korff04.htm.

90.   Korff and Kocis.

91.   Ibid.; Long, p. 351.

92.   Korff and Kocis; Long, p. 346.

93.   Korff and Kocis.

94.   The Bigfoot Forums, http://www.bigfootforums.com/index.php? showtopic=9999&mode=threaded&pid=199455.

95.   "The Patterson Film: A Discussion by Daniel Perez," Bigfoot Encounters, http://www.bigfootencounters.com/articles/forteantimes05.htm.

96.   Loren Coleman, Fate (May 2004), pp. 82-3.

97.   Dmitri Bayanov and Igor Burtsev, unpublished letter to Skeptical Inquirer (30 July 2004), Bigfoot Encounters, http://www.bigfootencounters.com/articles/response_si.htm.

98.   John Green, unpublished letter to Skeptical Inquirer (25 July 2004), Bigfoot Encounters, http://www.bigfootencounters.com/articles/response_si.htm.

99.   Ibid.

100.   Kal Korff, "Korff Statement About The Patterson Bigfoot Film Commentary," Rense.com (8 March 2004), http://www.rense.com/general50/kr.htm; Prometheus Books brochure for The Making of Bigfoot, March 2004; Prometheus Books (28 July 2010), http://www.prometheusbooks.com/index.php? main_page=product_info&cPath=43_147&products_id=1037100.

101.   Kal Korff, "Korff Statement About The Patterson Bigfoot Film Commentary."

102.   "Statement From Author Greg Long On Patterson Film," Rense.com (8 March 2004), http://www.rense.com/general50/statement.htm.

103.   Ibid.

104.   Amazon.com, http://www.amazon.com/Secret-Wars-Kal-K-Korff/dp/1591021499/ref=sr_1_1?s=books&ie=UTF8&qid=1280316287&sr=1-1.

105.   "Statement From Author Greg Long On Patterson Film."

106.   Kal Korff email to John Green (3 March 2004), Bigfoot Encounters, http://www.bigfootencounters.com/articles/response_si.htm.

107.   Greg Long email to Dmitri Bayanov and others, posted to the Forest Giants newsgroup on 23 May 2004.

108.   Kal Korff, "About Us," CriticalThinkers.org, http://www.kalkorff.com.

109.   Korff, "Korff Statement About The Patterson Bigfoot Film Commentary"; "Bigfoot" title search, Amazon.com (28 July 2010), http://www.amazon.com/s/ref=nb_sb_noss? url=search-alias%3Dus-stripbooks-tree&field-keywords=bigfoot&ih=6_0_0_0_1_0_0_0_0_1.109_163&fsc=-1&x=12&y=19.

6.
Marmaduke's Revenge

The Loch

Loch Ness is almost certainly the world's most famous "monster" lake. Located in the scenic Scottish Highlands, it measures 22.6 miles long and 1.7 miles across at its widest point. Its average depth is 433 feet, with a maximum official depth of 744.6 feet—although soundings taken by the submersible *Pisces* in 1969 suggest a true depth of 975 feet. With a surface area of 21.8 square miles, it is Scotland's second-largest lake (after Loch Lomond). By volume— 1.8 cubic miles, or 263 billion cubic feet—Loch Ness holds more water than all lakes in England and Wales combined. Tour guides aboard the *Royal Scot,* operating out of Fort Augustus, claim the loch's dark waters could submerge Earth's entire human population three times over.[1]

In short, it would appear that almost *anything* could hide within Loch Ness. And yet ....

Author Ronald Binns, writing in 1983, claimed that the first "announcement of a monster in 1930 flopped," because "no-one who lived around Loch Ness seemed ever to have heard of, let alone seen the monster."[2] We'll examine Binns and his work more closely, later in this chapter, but that statement should suffice to test his credibility for now.

Scottish historian Norton Newton—no relation to this author—claims that ancient Picts were the first people to record sightings of "Nessie," in prehistoric rock paintings of a creature commonly called the Pictish Beast or Pictish Elephant. The first specific sighting, dismissed by skeptics as mythical, dates from around 565 C.E., when Irish missionary Saint Columba allegedly invoked God's name to repel an aquatic monster near the mouth of the River Ness. Author Henry Bauer, former dean of Virginia Polytechnic Institute and State University's College of Arts and Sciences, has catalogued a minimum of forty-five eyewitness sightings from Loch Ness, reported between 1520 and 1930.[3] Clearly, whether Saint Columba's meeting with the beast is factual or legendary, Binns was wildly off the mark in claiming that no locals ever saw or heard of cryptids in the loch.

Continuing with Binns, he tells us that the second "announcement of a monster in 1933 proved a dazzling success." The reasons for that triumph, he says, were twofold. First, "one of the hottest summers of the century" produced "mirages and distortions due to heat-haze" on the water, certainly a possibility at any lake under the right conditions. Second, on 22 July, a couple of tourists from London, Mr. and Mrs. George Spicer, had "a frightening experience with an otter on a lonely road," prompting George to write "a melodramatic letter" to the *Inverness Courier*. According to Binns, that letter "inspired a tiny handful of other sightings by impressionable teenage girls, passing tourists, and local eccentrics." Thus, Binns says, "the Loch Ness mystery was given a new lease on life, and the monster myth has survived to the present day."[4]

Simple. If only it were true.

In fact, thanks to Professor Bauer, we know that 1933 produced at least twenty-one sightings of Nessie *before* the Spicers' encounter, beginning in January, with a minimum of sixty-nine more reported from 26 July through year's end.[5] How many cases constitute "a tiny handful"? Putting that aside, we should note that the Spicers described "a most extraordinary form of animal," elephant-gray, with a "trunk" or long neck, standing four feet high from the pavement and spanning a road twelve feet wide. Was it, as Binns insists, an otter distorted by heat haze? Or was it a "huddle of deer," as proposed by author Rupert Gould, forty-nine years earlier?[6] We may never know, but it seems safe to say that Binns has proved himself distinctly unreliable in summarizing facts.

"A Matter for Further Inquiry"
On 13 November 1933, Hugh Gray of Foyers snapped the first alleged photo of Nessie. It appeared in both the *Daily Record* and the *Daily Sketch* on 6 December, accompanied by statements from Kodak Company spokesmen declaring that the negative had not been tampered with. Six days later, Malcolm Irvine shot the first motion picture footage of an apparent cryptid in Loch Ness, from a hillside opposite Urquhart Castle. London's *Daily Mail* promptly announced that it would launch a "special mission of investigation" led by big-game hunter Marmaduke Wetherell, accompanied by reporter F. W. Memory and two photographers, Gustave Pauli and W. R. Turner.[7]

At first glance, "Duke" Wetherell seemed the ideal choice for point man on a monster hunt. Yorkshire born in 1886, he had fought in the Boer War, then used a £30,000 inheritance to build a 250-acre farm in Northern Rhodesia (now Zambia). He married an actress with four sons from a prior marriage, then sired a son and daughter of his own. Selling off the farm when stepson Christian Spurling suffered a bout of ill health, Wetherell moved the family to Johannesburg in 1916, spending a year with an outfit called African Film Productions, then returned alone to London in 1917, finally retrieving his wife and children four years later. His time in Africa left Wetherell smitten with hunting, photography and adventure. During the 1920s he directed films including *Wee MacGregor's Sweetheart* (1922), *His Wife's Husband* (1922), *Through Fire and Water* (1923), *Curfew Must Not Ring Tonight* (1923), *Darkness* (1923), *Women and Diamonds* (1924), *Livingstone* (1925), and *Robinson Crusoe* (1927).[8]

Wetherell's hunting party reached Inverness on 15 December and began patrolling Loch Ness by boat four days later. That same day—19 December—Wetherell reported finding white stains on the shore between Dores and Foyers, similar to those he recalled from African lakes occupied by hippopotamuses. On 20 December Wetherell announced discovery of large footprints ashore, between Foyers and Fort Augustus, returning to cast them in plaster the following day. The *Daily Mail* celebrated that find on 21 December with a headline reading: "Monster of Loch Ness is Not a Legend but a Fact."[9] That day's story quoted Wetherell as saying:

> "It is a four-fingered beast and it has feet or pads about eight inches across. I should judge it to be a very powerful soft-footed animal about 20 feet long. The spoor I have found clearly shows the undulations of the pads and the outlines of the claws and nails....I am convinced it can breathe like a hippopotamus or crocodile with just one nostril out of the water. The spoor I found is only a few hours old, clearly demonstrating that the animal is in the neighborhood where I expected to find it".[10]

While *The Times* of London snorted in ridicule, Wetherell broadcast his findings over the BBC on 23 December, his lecture introduced as "something to freeze your blood." One week later, on 30 December, Gustave Pauli packed the casts and shipped them to the *Daily Mail.* The crate arrived on 31 December, and was delivered to the Natural History Museum on New Year's Day.[11] Any fears of frozen blood evaporated on 4 January, when museum spokesmen W. T. Calman (Keeper of Zoology) and M. A. C. Hinton (Deputy Keeper of Zoology) announced their findings.

> "We are unable to find any significant difference between these impressions and those made by one foot of a hippopotamus. The closest agreement is with the right hind foot of a mounted specimen, probably not quite full grown. By the courtesy of the Superintendent of the Zoological Gardens, it has been possible to take a cast of the impression made by the same foot of a living female.
>
> In the general character this impression also agrees with the Loch Ness footprints, but the impressions left by the fleshy portions of the sole are much fuller and more rounded than in the case of the dried mounted specimen or of the Loch Ness footprints.[12]

And so the mystery was solved—almost. For years, most authors claimed the tracks were faked using a hippo's-foot umbrella stand owned by some unidentified local, without specifically blaming Duke Wetherell. Only long afterward was the true object identified as an ashtray from Wetherell's own trophy collection.[13]

The *Daily Mail* dusted off its battered reputation, declaring that the museum's finding "deepens further the mystery," leaving Nessie's existence "a matter for further inquiry." On 5 January 1934 witness Arthur Grant reported his encounter with an unknown creature on a road near Abriachan. Wetherell and Pauli rushed to that scene, as the *Daily Mail* reported discovery of a mangled roe deer on the loch's shore. Its carcass, the paper said, "looked as if it had been mauled by some huge animal."[14]

Rather curiously, even as it ran that news, the paper advanced a new theory, suggesting that Nessie might be a "particularly large gray seal." F. W. Memory's new dispatches hewed to that theme, while omitting any mention of Duke Wetherell—until 15 June, when the expedition's leader claimed his own sighting of the monster. It was certainly a giant seal, he said. Its head and neck protruded four feet six inches above the loch's surface, while the trailing hump of its back rose eighteen inches to two feet above water.[15]

That same day, the *Daily Mail* passed judgment on the Loch Ness mystery. "The only thing which will settle the whole matter," the paper editorialized, "is a photograph of the creature showing its head, so that the experts can definitely classify it."[16]

Caught on Film?

Ninety-six days later, on 21 April 1934, the hoped-for photograph was published on the *Daily Mail*'s front page. It had been snapped, the paper said, by Dr. Robert Kenneth Wilson, a gynecologist with offices on London's Queen Anne Street. According to Wilson, he and a friend—Maurice Chambers, of Thornbury—were en route to a wild-fowl shooting lease near Inverness, driving along the west shore of Loch Ness "around midday," when they noted "a sudden commotion in the water" some 150 to 200 yards offshore. Wilson saw "the head of some strange animal rising up out of the water" and stopped, grabbing a camera and snapping four quarter-plates while the object was visible. When it submerged, they pressed on to Inverness and delivered the plates to Ogston's, a chemist, where they were developed by George Morrison. Two of the plates were blank; one showed something resembling a swan's neck in profile; and the fourth framed something like a head preparing to submerge.[17]

For decades after the event, published accounts of the event habitually referred to Dr. Wilson's "excellent reputation." Eric Parker, then editor of *The Field*—the world's oldest country and field sports magazine, published continuously since 1853—was a close friend of Wilson's, describing him as "a man of unquestioned character and veracity." Wilson held Bachelor of Medicine and Bachelor of Surgery degrees from Cambridge, was a Fellow of the Royal College of Surgeons, and during World War II would serve as a lieutenant colonel in the Royal Artillery—none of which, it need hardly be said, precludes participation in a prank or practical joke.[18] Nonetheless, his reputation is worth noting, more particularly in regard to certain charges leveled at him posthumously.

Controversies surrounding the "surgeon's photograph" of Nessie begin with the date when it— or, more properly, *they*—were taken. Wilson himself never gave a specific date, but his first interviews on the subject appeared in the *Daily Mail* and the *Inverness Courier* on 20 April 1934, the day before his most famous photo was published. That suggests the sighting probably occurred on 18 or 19 April, and Henry Bauer's book on Nessie opts for the 19th—

although, three pages earlier, he cites the date as April 1st.[19] The latter date—with its suggestion of an "April Fool's Day" prank—had been "rumored" by the early 1970s, was stated as fact by Roy Mackal and television's *In Search Of* series by 1976, was echoed by author Paul Harrison in 1999, and is currently accepted as fact by John Kirk, a self-described Nessie believer and founding member of the British Columbia Scientific Cryptozoology Club.[20] Meanwhile, skeptic Steuart Campbell lists the date as 19 April, while Nicholas Witchell, based on correspondence with Dr. Wilson, settles for "early April."[21]

While the "rumored" date of April 1st assumes significance for superficial skofftic treatments of the subject, then, nothing supports it factually. And, as we shall see, the date turns out to be irrelevant in the most widely-touted allegation of a fraud. What matters most are details of the photographs themselves.

How Big? How Far?
Dr. Wilson's impressions of Nessie were reported to the world on 20 April 1934. He told the *Daily Mail,* "I saw a long neck about three feet out of the water and a head which looked small; but I was so hurried that I cannot describe it well." And, to the *Inverness Courier*: "What I really saw was an object with a swan-like neck, almost three feet out of the water. The head was small, but, as I said, I really had no chance of making an accurate observation in my hurry to get some 'snaps.'" While other details of his story varied with the passage of a quarter-century, Wilson never altered his description of the object he observed and photographed.[22] It remained for various observers of the photo to support or contradict the three-foot estimate from calculations of their own, with widely disparate results.

Longtime monster-hunter Tim Dinsdale, writing in 1960, analyzed rings and ripples surrounding the upraised object in Wilson's photo, and while he produced no estimate of size, he came away convinced that "the picture is not a fake." Nearly two decades later, influenced by "rumors" of an April Fool's Day hoax, Dinsdale reluctantly admitted that "the ripples which had influenced me so strongly could have been caused by someone throwing stones." How that might have affected the photograph's subject, animate or otherwise, remained unexplained.[23]

Another opinion from 1960, advanced to author Maurice Burton by one A. J. Wells, declared: "It is assumed that the length of the neck of the creature in the picture is 5-6 feet, but the nature of the various sets of ripples indicate to me that the scale is in fact very much smaller than that. Most people can tell distressingly easily, in film sequences of naval battles re-enacted with models, for instance, that what they are looking at are models and not real ships, not because they look different but because the waves that surround the models look quite different to life-sized waves. In other words, ripples like this just look different to waves, and are not merely different in scale. My experience in this direction would suggest to me that the neck of the creature in the photograph is not 5-6 feet long but 9 inches to 1 foot long....I think it is much smaller than some people imagine."[24]

Wells, whose qualifications pass unmentioned, failed to say whose estimated measurement of five to six feet he was contradicting. Whether or not one "believes" in Nessie, I submit that some more formal process is required to judge the object's size, beyond simply claiming that particular waves "just look different."

Meanwhile, the recipient of Wells's wisdom—British zoologist and popular science writer Maurice Burton—underwent a literal sea change in his opinion of Nessie. Writing of the Wilson photo in the *Illustrated London News,* on 20 February 1959, Burton said: "If this photograph is genuine, as I am now convinced beyond all doubt it is, then there is no argument about the reality of the Loch Ness Monster, nor any doubt of its being a large animate body." Nine months later, in a letter dated 29 October, Burton wrote: "I have come to the conclusion that it is probably a plesiosaur-type animal." Something changed radically over the next year, and his final word on the subject—*The Elusive Monster* (1961)—dismissed Wilson's photo as a snapshot of a diving otter's tail. Perhaps embarrassed by his own reversal, Burton wrote, on 30 April 1962: "I am now very resentful of those who, wittingly or unwittingly, have misled us and have caused me to spend so much time and effort needlessly, and to make me look ridiculous."[25]

Nicholas Witchell offered an "interesting postscript" to the Wilson photo, in the 1984 edition of his book *The Loch Ness Story.* There, he stated that "in 1972 the better picture was submitted to the computer-enhancement process used by America's National Aeronautic and Space Administration on the *Apollo* moon photographs....The improved picture showed definite signs of 'whiskers' hanging down from the animal's lower jaw and must finally remove any lingering doubts about the authenticity of this photograph."[26] Fourteen years later, in September 1998, the BBC's *X Creatures* echoed that story, reporting that Wilson's photo had been enhanced at NASA's Jet Propulsion Laboratory in California.[27] In fact, while Witchell referred specifically to NASA enhancement of the "surgeon's photo," no documentation of any such treatment has yet been produced. In retrospect, it seems that Witchell garbled an account of NASA's work on the controversial "flipper" photo, snapped in 1972 by an underwater camera at Loch Ness, further confused with a "gargoyle head" photo taken underwater in 1975.[28]

Next up with a verdict on the Wilson photo, in 1976, was Dr. Roy Mackal, director of the Loch Ness Investigation Bureau from 1966 to 1972. While supporting the existence of large cryptids in the loch, he agreed with Maurice Burton that the Wilson photograph did not depict a monster. Rather than a diving otter's tail, however, Mackal thought the creature was a bird of indeterminate species. That conclusion—which he changed twelve years later—was "based on [his] own observations of diving birds in the general area where Wilson took his pictures."[29]

In August 1981, at a Vermont conference on Lake Champlain's supposed cryptids, J. Richard Greenwell of the ISC compared the Wilson photo to an alleged snapshot of "Champ" taken by Sandra Mansi in 1977 (see Chapter 2). With tracings of the objects from both photos, Greenwell noted that "when you align them a certain way, you find that the head configurations are very similar." Furthermore, "we find that the two necks are practically identical in size"—whatever that might be. "And again," he added, "not only do you find them similar, but the whole head to neck ratio is very much the same in both animals."[30]

Enter Ronald Binns, whose treatise *The Loch Ness Mystery Solved* was published in Britain in 1983, appearing in the United States a year later. That tome included claims that Nessie was unknown even to locals before 1930, making it "the last great modern myth"; that monster movies such as *The Lost World* (1924) and *King Kong* (1933) paved the way for a hoax; that monster-hunters "often have no formal education, and they revel in their amateur status," being "cheerfully ignorant of zoology, natural history, human psychology or even the history and ecology of Loch Ness itself"; and that "Loch Ness monster addicts are...incurable romantics," whose efforts have "now taken on the overtones of a fringe religion."[31] And speaking of psychology (without revealing his credentials in that field), Binns opined that—

> "Monster-hunters can never quite bring themselves to admit what their jumbled motives are in devoting their time to the pursuit of a mythical beast. When pressed on the subject they usually talk in highminded tones about the great need for "conservation" of those wonderful and rare animals....There is something slightly absurd and comical about such tender concern, in view of the monster's astonishingly elusive nature. Psychology is not something the believers care to know about.[32]

So, who is Ronald Binns? One of his editors reports that Binns "has visited the loch since the 1960s and studied the evidence that has emerged over the last fifty years."[33] Authors Elizabeth Campbell and David Solomon describe Binns more specifically, from personal acquaintance, as a member of the monster-hunting Loch Morar Survey in the early 1970s, at which time he was "an arts graduate reading for an M.Phil. [Master of Philosophy]." On the night of 10 August 1971, Binns and companion Ian Johnson (a doctoral candidate in biology) reported sighting an unexplained wake on dead-calm Loch Morar, which they pursued in a Zodiac boat at full throttle.[34]

Rather than speculate on Binns's education or his mental state, as he does when attacking others, let reviewers of his work speak for themselves. Dr. Henry Bauer deemed the Binns book "an exemplar of specious reasoning."[35] Adrian Shine, another acquaintance of Binns in his role as director of the Loch Ness and Morar Project, was more specific—and more scathing—when he reviewed the book in 1985, for the ISC's journal *Cryptozoology*, identifying Binns as "a former believer" who abandoned active field research in 1972 and "who now reaches an opposite and uncompromising conclusion."[36] While praising some aspects of Binns's work, Shine noted the following problems:

- Misstatement of facts, as "[w]hen dealing with the Academy of Applied Sciences underwater results of 1972...Binns states that the camera was triggered by the sonar, when, in fact, there was no connection between the two."[37]
- Fabrication and use of false analogies: "Having discarded his chance of making a valid criticism [of the underwater photos], he is reduced to suggesting that the area was 'frequented by frogmen,' and that this is a good time to discuss the Piltdown Man hoax."[38]

- Arguing from ignorance: "When discussing sonar, the best Binns can suggest is that it doesn't work. In cataloging the various reports, it is clear that he is simply out of his depth. Not only does he make numerous errors of detail, but misses most relevant clues to what would have been valid criticisms."[39]
- And again: "This second half of the book dealing with evidence, though well written, betrays a lack of technical knowledge, a shortage of practical research, and a complete ignorance of current attitudes."[40]
- Worse still: "The attack upon former comrades-in-arms has a bitterness which spills over into the rest of the work. Clearly, if there is no monster, then all evidence must be accounted for somehow, and human frailties must answer for a great deal, but Binns unfortunately seems to prefer personal innuendo than to an assessment of material."[41]
- Finally, Shine found Binns driven by "a jealous determination to be seen alone in [his] conclusions," to the point that he either ignores previous skeptical reports on Nessie or attacks authors like Maurice Burton—who beat him to the punch by twenty-two years—on the basis of ephemeral errors.[42]

Next up to scrutinize the Wilson photo was Steuart Campbell, whose Web site describes him as a former architect, laid off in the 1970s, who then "studied with the Open University, gaining a BA in 1983 (mainly science and mathematics) and in the 1980s I took up writing." His first book was *The Loch Ness Monster: The Evidence,* published in 1986. Three more have followed, plus "over 130 articles on diverse subjects, mainly investigations of one sort or another, and very many letters to the press." Campbell's Wikipedia page calls him "an Edinburgh-based skeptic and investigative science writer" whose work focuses chiefly on "science and pseudoscience-related matters."[43]

Before Campbell's full-length book on Nessie surfaced, he fired an opening salvo in the *British Journal of Photography,* published on 20 April 1984 under the title "The Surgeon's Monster Hoax." After locating the original uncropped print, previously unpublished, Campbell calculated that the object depicted was only twenty-eight inches tall, thus "a rather small monster!" As for Wilson's second snapshot, Campbell opined, "It can hardly be an accident that this second picture, which might have revealed the true nature of the object, is out of focus."[44] Campbell's book, published two years later, noted that published explanations for the photo's subject include "a large tree root brought to the surface by convection currents or gas bubbles, a diving bird, such as a crested grebe, the pectoral fin of a 'sick pilot whale,' and the tail of an otter."[45]

Paul LeBlond and Michael Collins, from the University of British Columbia's Department of Oceanography, brought greater expertise to their analysis of Wilson's famous photo in 1987. Using the same technique employed in their analysis of Sandra Mansi's "Champ" photo five years earlier, and working from the same uncropped original print used by Campbell, they determined that the shape observed in Wilson's famous shot stood four feet above the loch's surface.[46] Based on that conclusion, and on Richard Greenwell's earlier comparison of the Wilson and Mansi photos, Roy Mackal renounced his previous opinion, stating that "I now accept what many others have proposed all along: that at least one of the Wilson photographs represents a large unidentified animal in Loch Ness." Furthermore, he wrote, "The similarity between the two objects demonstrated by Greenwell supports my new conclusion that the unidentified animals photographed in Lake Champlain and Loch Ness represent one and the same species."[47]

Steuart Campbell would have none of it. He found the "laudable attempt" by Collins and LeBlond "flawed by one major defect, and perhaps by some minor ones too." Specifically, he claimed, their calculation of the day's prevailing wind was insupportable, concluding that the photo's subject was "indeed an otter's tail." Dr. LeBlond contested Campbell's claims concerning windage on 19 April 1934 and the angle of Wilson's camera, propelling their debate into another year. In round two, Campbell claimed that Wilson's photograph had been reversed, a new and wholly unsupported theory which LeBlond rightly branded inconsistent "with the observations and his [Campbell's] previous analyses."[48]

Conspiracy?
Long before that debate unfolded, on 7 December 1975, London's *Sunday Telegraph* published an article alleging that the Wilson photo was an outright hoax. Columnist "Mandrake"—né Philip Purser—claimed that he had tracked Marmaduke Wetherell's son, Ian, to a pub he owned in Chelsea. There, Ian described the fraud and its motive as follows, according to Purser.

> "The Loch Ness monster was one of the great silly season standbys at that time. My father, Marmaduke Wetherell, was a fairly well-known big-game hunter. The Mail commissioned him to look for the monster, using Asdic [sonar] equipment and so on. When he reported—as he had expected—that there were no signs of life, they seemed rather peeved.
>
> So my father said, "All right, we'll give them their monster." I remember that we drove up to Scotland again in my Hillman. There was a friend of his called Chambers, an insurance broker—they're both dead now. I had the camera, which was a Leica, and still rather a novelty then.
>
> Chambers had a shoot on one side of the Loch. He was the one who sent off the pictures—actually the undeveloped strip of film, saying he'd seen the creature while out shooting and tried to snap it. In fact we made it from one of the little toy submarines you could buy for about half-a-crown, plus some rubber tubing and what-have-you. It was only a few inches high.
>
> We found an inlet where the tiny ripples would look like full size waves out on the loch, and with the actual scenery in the background. Then it was just a matter of winding up the sub and getting it to dive just below the surface so the neck and head

drew a proper little V in the water.

I took about five shots with the Leica, then suddenly a water bailiff turned up. I suppose he had heard voices and thought we were fishing. Dad put his foot on the monster and sank it, and that was that".[49]

Well, not quite. While "Mandrake's" article inspired the most aggressive attack on Wilson's photo, it—and Ian Wetherell's confession—contain major discrepancies. The Duke's son led with lies about his father's expedition using sonar and reporting "no signs of life" from the loch, omitted the hippo-foot hoax, and pretended that the *Daily Mail* was simply "peeved" by Duke's failure to obtain results. Beyond that, Ian lied about the photograph itself. The Leica he referred to, with its "strip of film," did not use the 3⅛×4⅛-inch "quarter-plate" tintypes that produced Wilson's photos. The photos displayed no "proper little V in the water," nor any "actual scenery in the background" beyond a narrow strip of distant shoreline. Author "Mandrake" compounded those glaring mistakes with his own false claims that the published photo included "[in] the distance...the familiar shoreline and mountains," while a nonexistent caption "gave the exact time and place" where the photo was snapped. Stranger still, he wrote, "Alas, there were no further sightings" of Nessie after Wilson's photo made the papers![50] Dr. Bauer's chronicle lists ninety-nine for the remaining months of 1934 alone.[51]

For all its sensational claims, the "Mandrake" article passed largely unnoticed in 1975. Ronald Binns raised the next allegation of conspiracy in 1983, with a claim that "In later years, Wilson's youngest son bluntly admitted that his father's pictures were fraudulent."[52] Wilson's harshest critics, David Martin and Alastair Boyd, reluctantly admit that "[t]here appears to be no substantiating evidence to support this statement." They attribute it to a letter written to Tim Dinsdale by Dr. Wilson's sister-in-law in February 1979, quoting one line out of context that read: "Col. Wilson's younger son, tragically drowned in the Solway [Firth] several years ago was very sceptical over the whole Loch Ness question, and he told a cousin it was a hoax!"[53] Without cherry-picking, however, the letter presents a rather different picture.

"I have made enquiries from my husband's family about the "Surgeon's Photo." His nephew with whom he had quite a lot to do says as far as he understood the photo was genuine, and he has had no doubts. Col. Wilson's younger son, tragically drowned in the Solway several years ago was very sceptical over the whole Loch Ness question, and he told a cousin it was a hoax! At the time it was taken, he was much too young to appreciate it, and sons are often critical of their parents' achievements.

The other relative, a niece, well remembers the time the photo was taken and how her uncle was so excited about it and told his sister (her mother) exactly the conditions when it was taken. She does not think how he behaved threw any doubt on the authenticity. She was surprised to hear that doubt had arisen".[54]

Clearly, no proof of fraud—nor even serious support for Boyd and Martin when they write that "Certainly the [Wilson] family were divided in their opinions."[55]

It was the "Mandrake" article that finally propelled Martin and Boyd in their attack on Wilson. They deem it "suspicious" that the error-laden story failed to launch a hue and cry in 1975, yet Adrian Shine himself only stumbled on the article by chance in December 1990, fifteen years after the fact. By the time Martin learned of the story and went seeking Ian Wetherell, in January 1991, the Duke's son had been dead for five years. A month later, however, he struck gold after a fashion, with Ian's aging half-brother, Christian Spurling.[56]

Spurling was a certified "character." Born in 1906, the son of acclaimed marine artist John Charles Robert "Jack" Spurling (1870-1933), he moved to Africa with his mother, siblings, and step-father Marmaduke Wetherell at age six, and nearly died from blackwater fever (a complication of malaria) at ten. Spurling went to sea for the first time at age eighteen, served as a constable during Britain's nine-day general strike in May 1926, then moved to Malaya the following month, to work on a rubber plantation. Captured by the Japanese in 1937, he spent three and a half years in jungle prison camps. Back in London at war's end, he worked at processing and editing film for George Humphries and Company until 1963, when he retired to Worthing and followed in his father's footsteps as an artist.[57]

David Martin—a teacher and zoologist with Adrian Shine's Loch Ness and Morar Project since 1981—interviewed Spurling for the first time in February 1991, then returned for a second chat with partner Alastair Boyd in July 1992. Boyd is interesting in his own right, having logged a Nessie sighting with wife Sue at Urquhart Bay on 30 July 1979. They saw Nessie for about five seconds, from 150 yards, describing the creature as twenty feet long and moving forward "in a rolling motion like a whale." Boyd describes himself as "a Loch Ness researcher whose particular specialty is photographic and eyewitness evidence of Nessie."[58]

The story Christian Spurling told to Boyd and Martin was remarkable. Spinning off from the late Ian Wetherell's inaccurate account of why his father dreamed up yet another hoax, Spurling reported a phone call from Marmaduke, asking, "Christian, can you make me a monster?" Ian allegedly bought a toy submarine from F. S. Woolworth in Richmond, Surrey, and Spurling—proclaimed an expert model-maker in addition to his other skills—spent eight days crafting a miniature Nessie from "plastic wood," fourteen inches long, with a twelve-inch arching neck. Stabilized with a strip of lead soldered to its keel, the contraption "was designed to sail partially submerged, just showing the conning tower and part of the superstructure." That accomplished, Spurling and the Wetherells allegedly drove to some unspecified point on the shore of Loch Ness and snapped their photos as described in the 1975 "Mandrake" column, subsequently recruiting Dr. Wilson as "a stooge" through mutual friend Maurice Chambers. According to Martin and Boyd, "Wilson actually had no connection with the photography beyond taking the plates to be developed by a chemist in Inverness and selling the photographs to the *Daily Mail*."[59]

At this point, let's recall the "Mandrake" article, wherein Ian Wetherell claimed the photos were printed from a "strip of film," not the actual plates—and that *Chambers* sent the film to be developed. Spurling had already contradicted two key points of the initial conspiracy tale, but as we shall see, Boyd and Martin accepted *both* versions as true. Stranger yet, Spurling could not even recall the year when the hoax was perpetrated. His "signed confession," scrawled on a print of the surgeon's photo, reads: "This is a photograph of the 'monster' made by me in 1933/34 for M. A. Wetherell."[60]

Having procured the crypto-scoop of a lifetime, Boyd and Martin sat on it for twenty months. Their explanation for that lapse is that "[w]e deliberately timed the article to coincide as closely as possible to the 60th Anniversary [*sic*] of the original publication in the *Daily Mail*." And yet, they broke the story in the *Sunday Telegraph* on 13 March 1994, a full thirty-nine days before said anniversary. Odd timing—and clearly not "as close as possible"—but the delay accomplished one thing: Christian Spurling died before its publication, in November 1993, and thus was rendered safe from cross-examination.[61]

Announcement of the hoax made global headlines, and spawned more myths in the process. John Darnton, writing for the *New York Times* on 20 March 1994, was relatively sedate, although he managed to peg the price of Spurling's toy submarine—two shillings, six pence— with remarkable precision. He also garbled Duke Wetherell's initial hoax, alluding to a nonexistent hippo-foot umbrella stand, then closed with David Martin's assurance that Nessie truly exists after all: "There are thousands of eyewitness accounts, and they cannot be taken away."[62]

People magazine added its two cents on 28 March, repeating the umbrella-stand fable with "dinosaur-size footprints" thrown in for good measure. The anonymous story also pioneered false claims that Spurling "confessed" on his death-bed, alleging that Martin and Boyd "got the truth out of him not long before his death at age 90 last November." Finally, it closed by saying, "Boyd and Martin still believe there is a Nessie. Boyd says he saw her in 1979. Now they know there's a fake Nessie out there too. When old Wetherell noticed a member of the lake patrol approaching, he scuttled the little monster in the banks of Loch Ness [*sic*]."[63] Needless to say, no one was looking for the model, sixty years after the fact. And it was just as well, since Spurling, while he lived, had no idea where the alleged photo shoot had occurred.

"Positively Perverse"
Readers noted fault lines in the Spurling tale and cited them in print. One issue was the use of "plastic wood" to build the mini-Nessie mounted on a clockwork submarine. Questions were raised concerning its availability in 1934, and while the product sold today under that trademarked name by DAP Products Inc. did not exist, it seems that Spurling had referred to some generic form of putty which, he said, required eight days to dry.[64]

Next up, the submarine itself. Spurling scoured catalogs of antique toys and never found one matching the dimensions that he cited for his model—nor have I, in research spanning seven years—but he eventually settled a version of "the type," while noting that his own "would be a little thinner."[65] Let us grant the obvious, that wind-up clockwork submarines existed in the

1930s, and move on to more substantive arguments.

Filmmaker Richard Smith was first in print with a critique of the Spurling hoax claim, writing for *Fate* magazine in November 1995. He summarized the arguments already listed in this chapter, noting that the uncropped surgeon's photo refutes any claim that the picture was taken in "an inlet where the tiny ripples would look like full-sized waves," and further questioning the claim that Duke Wetherell sank the model after a water bailiff turned up unexpectedly, thereby conveniently eradicating any physical evidence of the prank.[66]

Joe Nickell rose to Spurling's defense in the March 1996 issue of *Skeptical Inquirer,* leading with a dose of guilt by association. *Fate,* he archly noted, is "a magazine that promotes belief in paranormal topics." Worse yet, Smith's piece "was sandwiched between a testimonial, 'My Glimpse of Bigfoot,' and an article suggesting that 'alien technology' was responsible for the strange hybrid creatures of Greek mythology."[67] Nickell knows perfectly well that freelance authors have no say in where a magazine editor places their articles, and his implication that *Fate* prints only items "promoting belief" in the paranormal is simply false—as proved by my own article of March 2008, debunking an infamous sea-serpent hoax.[68]

Nickell himself misstated Spurling's case while trying to defend it, claiming that Duke Wetherell hatched the plot "with Dr. Wilson agreeing to take the photos," when Spurling and his spokesmen, Boyd and Martin, all maintained that Wilson never laid a finger on the camera or plates. After botching that critical point, Nickell wrote: "It seemed to me that Smith's points ranged from weak to dubious, but I decided to forego a response in hopes of soliciting a more expert opinion."[69] His chosen expert? Ronald Binns.

Binns favored Nickell with a three-page letter in December 1995. After "conceding that Smith's perceived faults with Spurling's story might suggest it was bogus," Binns wrote: "On the other hand, as Spurling was an old man when he was interviewed maybe he was just confused. After more than half a century anyone's memory would surely be unreliable. Maybe he was right about how the model was made but wrong about the dimensions. Maybe the model sank accidentally (as did the hugely expensive model monster made for the Billy Wilder film *The Private Life of Sherlock Holmes*.) Even if the object was 1.2 metres high, so what? It could still have been a model."[70]

"So what," indeed! To Binns and Nickell, it makes perfect sense for Spurling to be wildly off the mark on every major point of his elaborate conspiracy. Glaring discrepancies count only when applied to witnesses suggesting the existence of a cryptid. If Spurling can't recall the year, if he hallucinates a water bailiff's visit to the inlet he could never locate, if his memory shrinks a four-foot model by 75 percent—well, so what? The skofftic double-standard only demands pinpoint, unwavering accuracy from witnesses who claim cryptid sightings.

Addressing the second Wilson photo, Binns found his word for the day: "The second Wilson photograph *obviously* portrays a different object photographed in different weather conditions (and I suspect from a different angle). It may have been a cruder model, or it may have been a bird. If it is 'rarely seen,' as Smith claims, that is because it is a bad photo of a very dubious object. Since it *obviously* isn't the object shown in the more famous photo, the *obvious* question is how did Wilson manage to photograph two monsters?"[71] (My italics.)

What's "obvious" to Binns may elude other viewers of the photograph—even when he helps by "suspecting" different weather conditions and camera angles, or proposing a second "cruder model" never mentioned by Spurling, Martin, or Boyd. The possibility of a submerging neck and head does not occur to Binns, because he had concluded that all photos taken at the loch are faked by hoaxers. *Obviously.*

Continuing in the same vein, Binns wrote to Nickell: "Black and white photographs are so much easier to fake than colour photographs, and still photographs are so much easier to fake than home-movie or video film. The fact that the object shown in Wilson's photograph is very close to the shore is itself very suspicious, as this is just what one would expect from a model thrown into the loch. There is also almost what amounts to a basic rule about Nessie photos and films. The photos, being fakes and/or models, are always of an object relatively close to the photographer. The movie film, being genuine footage of an object which is not a monster, is always too far away to be properly identifiable."[72]

Leaving aside the assumption that all Nessie photos are "fakes and/or models," nothing substantiates Binns's claim that the object in Wilson's photo "is very close to the shore." No version of the photo displays any foreground at all.

Forging ahead, Binns wrote: "Richard D. Smith is wrong about the object not being photographed in an inlet. The part of the loch where Wilson said he took his photo consists of a series of inlets and there is no reason to suppose it wasn't photographed in one of these inlets."[73] Alas, as we've seen, Martin and Boyd deny that Wilson took the photos, while Spurling could never say *where* the shots were taken. And again, with no trace of a foreground in the picture, there is clearly "no reason to suppose" it *was* photographed in some hypothetical inlet.

Even the photo's composition rankled Binns: "Now that we have most of the original print what is surely striking is how the object photographed is more or less dead centre—rather too neatly and well composed for what is alleged to be an animal photographed by chance."[74] Which proves nothing in the world, except that someone *aimed* the camera directly at a thing he hoped to photograph. Would Binns be happier if Wilson's Nessie appeared at an edge of the frame, or off in a corner? Has he never seen any of several million nature photographs depicting creatures in the wild, "neatly and well composed"? We have already seen that he dismissed poorly-focused photos on those grounds alone. He is impossible to satisfy.

Finally, befitting a former student of philosophy, Nickell told his readers that "Binns concluded with some philosophical thoughts." Specifically: "I suspect after all this time we are never going to find out the full facts of the Wilson photo. The telling case against this and all the other Nessie photos is that in later years no one has ever managed to film the objects shown in either colour film, on a home-movie or on a video."[75]

If we may never learn "the full facts of the Wilson photo," should we assume that Binns doubts Spurling, after all? It hardly matters, since his claim that no color home-movies or videotapes of supposed Loch Ness monsters exist is patently false. The first color film from Loch Ness was shot by G. E. Taylor on 28 May 1938, followed by others in May and June 1967 (the latter acknowledged by Binns, thus contradicting himself), and in August 1977. The first purported videotape of Nessie was shot on 6 August 1983. Others have followed through the years.[76] Binns can only be correct if he demands that someone catch "the objects shown" in Wilson's photographs—same pose, same profile—on a color film or tape. Which might, indeed, be deemed suspicious.

Perhaps dissatisfied at last with the critique from Binns—although he would reprint it ten years later[77]—Nickell cast about for more "expert" support and found it in the person of Mike Hutchinson, whom Nickell identified as "the *Skeptical Inquirer*'s official and indefatigable representative in the United Kingdom." Concerning the Wilson photo, Hutchinson wrote: "[G]iven an explanation which fits virtually all the facts, and meshes in so neatly with what we know of Duke Wetherell (and the gullibility of tabloid newspaper editors) it seems positively perverse not to accept the Spurling account."[78]

My dictionary offers the following definitions for *perverse*: "1. Directed away from what is right or good; perverted; 2. Obstinately persisting in an error or fault; wrongly self-willed or stubborn; 3. Marked by a disposition to oppose and contradict; 4. Cranky; peevish." Any or all may apply, we presume, if one persists in contradicting stories filled with gaping holes and glaring contradictions. Conversely, by ignoring blatant gaffes, one is determined to be "right or good."

Richard Smith replied to Nickell with a letter to *S.I.*, which, unlike John Green's on the Patterson film (Chapter 5), was actually printed. Calling attention to "the unacceptable double standard applied during debates over cryptozoology," Smith questioned whether Martin, Boyd, and Nickell would have accepted Spurling's tale, delayed by six decades, if he had claimed that the Wilson photos were genuine. The obvious answer: "Of course not." Worse yet, Smith noted, "Binns and other apologists are ready to blithely modify Spurling's account whenever problems arise...until what should be consistent, definitive testimony becomes conveniently malleable." He further cited Nessie skeptic Steuart Campbell, who had penned a letter of his own to *S.I.* (published in the March/April 1995 issue), rejecting Spurling's tale with the observation that "[i]n their eagerness to undermine paranormal claims, writers in SI exhibit a tendency to accept any normal explanation, whether or not there is adequate evidence."[79]

Nickell replied in print that "[w]hat Richard Smith sees as an 'unacceptable double standard' is simply the necessary implementation of the maxim, 'Extraordinary claims require extraordinary proof.' This means one must have considerably more proof for the sighting of a sea monster than for that of a fish—or a sea-serpent model." Sidestepping Christian Spurling altogether, he pressed on: "While Smith attempts to cast doubt on details of the photo affair, the arguments of Binns and others are persuasive that the famous photograph is indeed a hoax....The points Smith raises range from the untrue to the dubious, as we have seen, and he is merely repeating himself." Nickell then repeats *him*self, quoting Mike Hutchinson to the effect that "it seems positively perverse not to accept the Spurling account."[80]

And so, at least for Nickell and *S.I.*, the case was closed.

"We Were All Anti-him"

Five years after their exposé initially grabbed headlines, Martin and Boyd expanded their tale in a short self-published book. The long delay remains unexplained: perhaps the authors spent their time in fruitless pursuit of a commercial publisher, or other business may have stalled their writing to a rate of one page per month. Another possibility is that they may have needed time to dig up dirt on Dr. Wilson, since nearly two-thirds of their slender tome is aimed at blackening his reputation.

That work was undertaken first by other hands, on 21 July 1995, when the FilmRoos company aired an episode of its *Ancient Mysteries* program dealing with Nessie on the A&E Network. During that broadcast, the producers falsely claimed that exposure of the photo hoax caused Dr. Wilson such embarrassment that he fled England for Papua New Guinea, later dying in Australia. In fact, he *did* die Down Under—but in 1969, a full quarter-century before Christian Spurling's "confession."[81]

Using the double standard noted by Richard Smith and denied by Joe Nickell, Boyd and Martin listed various "discrepancies" between the stories told by Wilson in 1934 and 1957, with a separate column dated 1989 (twenty years after Wilson's demise) for comments quoted by Nicholas Witchell. Among the so-called gaffes, Wilson deviated on whether the photo was taken at midday or morning; whether the object was 100 to 300 yards offshore (1934), or 200 to 300 yards (1957); whether he owned the camera or it was borrowed from a friend; and whether he saw "a sudden commotion in the water" (1934) or watched "for a minute" before the object rose (1957). They pay particular attention to his statements that "I was so excited I did not pause to observe it properly; what it is I do not pretend to know" (1934) and "I could not say what it was" (1957), which in fact do not contradict one another at all.[82]

All these, say Boyd and Martin, are significant discrepancies and indicators of deception. On the other hand, when Christian Spurling flubs and hedges every detail of his own confession ... well, so what?

From there, the authors launched their frontal assault on Dr. Wilson's character. They began with one Betty MacDougal—curator of Adrian Schine's former Official Loch Ness Monster Exhibition, no longer "official" in the wake of a £1.3 lawsuit, settled with a neighboring tourist attraction in June 2010[83]—who met Australian tourist Sonya Schembri, once employed by Wilson's aged son in Melbourne. Schembri subsequently wrote MacDougal a letter, we're told, stating that Dr. Wilson "was a great prankster with a wicked sense of humor," and that while he "didn't ever tell anyone, the generally held opinion amongst the family is they are sure [the photo] is probably a fake."[83]

Third-hand hearsay, contradicted by Wilson's sister-in-law years earlier, thus becomes "fact"—and there was worse to follow. Schembri also wrote that "Shortly after the photo was brought to light through the press, [Wilson] was brought before an official board of surgeons. I believe he was reprimanded about the photos and the press it had received and was given an ultimatum—a career in surgery or photography! So, surgery won out and obviously he kept quiet about his photo from then on!"[84]

She "believes" ... based on what? The tale of Dr. Wilson staying silent on the subject "from then on"—i.e., from 1934 onward—is patently false. Martin and Boyd themselves reprint letters he wrote to author Constance Whyte between 1955 and 1957, quoted in her book about the Loch Ness Monster, and to Maurice Burton in 1962.[85]

As for proof that Wilson was threatened with loss of his medical license in 1934, what have Boyd and Martin unearthed? They say: "The British Medical Council has confirmed to us in writing that Colonel Wilson was not struck off the Medical Register and continued his practice in various locations around the world."[86] In short, no proof at all.

Defeated on that front, Boyd and Martin proceed to trumpet discovery of Dr. Wilson's "open confession" to a hoax.[87] They begin with letters from the files of Maurice Burton, written in 1963-64, alluding to various anonymous informants. Among Burton's comments:

> "I was introduced some time ago to one of Wilson's close friends and he assured me that the whole thing was a hoax, a photograph of an artefact placed in the water.[88]
>
> [S]omeone got in touch with me to say that he was a personal friend of the Surgeon and that the picture was not what it was supposed to be.[89]
>
> I received a telephone call that took me to a London club where I met a close friend of Wilson who assured me that "everybody" in that club, of which Wilson had been...a member, knew the picture was a hoax....[H]e gave me the names of prominent men who would confirm what I said [sic].[90]

Oddly, Burton claimed, "I wrote to a few of these men and received guarded replies, as one might expect."[91] Why "guarded," one might ask, thirty years after a harmless prank in which the unnamed "prominent men" played no part beyond (allegedly) watching Wilson pat himself on the back? Even Boyd and Martin were dissatisfied, writing: "The net was closing on Wilson, but the evidence remained circumstantial and hearsay."[92]

Seeking solid proof, they settled on Major Norman Edwin Egginton. Sadly (or luckily) for Boyd and Martin, Egginton had died "about 1978," or else "disappeared without a trace," in an alternate account.[93] The authors thus were left to build a case, once more, from hearsay evidence.

First in the witness chair was Liverpool-born writer and criminologist Richard Whittington-Egan, a recognized expert on Jack the Ripper. Back in 1974, Whittington-Egan had written an article on Nessie for *The Contemporary Review,* stating that "a friend of the late Mr. Wilson has informed me that he was told by the Surgeon that the photograph was faked as a joke. Wilson, he added, had the reputation of being a great practical joker." Decades later, Whittington-Egan named Major Egginton as the friend and a fellow member of Wilson's unnamed club, where "apparently all the club members knew that the picture was a phoney."[93]

Egginton could no longer speak for himself, but he had penned two letters to teenage future-author Nicholas Witchell in November 1970, one stating that in 1940, during military service, Wilson "told three of us, quietly in the mess[,] how he and a friend had hoaxed the local inhabitants of Loch Ness. His friend with whom he used to fish the loch from time to time was a very keen amateur photographer who had taken a photograph of the loch and then at home had apparently superimposed a model of a monster on the plate. After this photograph was shown in the Loch Ness area, the press took up the matter and the resulting publicity according to 'R. K.' [Wilson] so scared them that it was kept very quiet."[94]

Voila! Proof positive—except for four glaring, fatal discrepancies.

First, the story of a "friend"—presumably Maurice Chambers—photographing an empty loch, then superimposing a monster on the plates at home, makes total hash of both Ian Wetherell's and Christian Spurling's accounts, claiming the model was photographed at Loch Ness and left there.

Second, Wilson's photos—remember the critical plural—were never "shown in the Loch Ness area" before their front-page newspaper publication.

Third, the press did not "take up the matter" after time had passed. By all accounts, Wilson himself was interviewed a day *before* the famous photograph appeared in print.

And finally, as we have seen, Dr. Wilson did not "keep very quiet" after April 1934, despite mythical threats to his livelihood from the British Medical Council.

Those minor points aside, Egginton's story was a perfect fit, described by Boyd and Martin as "the most important evidence against the Surgeon's Photograph that has ever come to light." In fact, they crowed, "like the Mandrake article, [it] provided sufficient lines of enquiry in which we ultimately substantiated all the claims."[95]

Well ... not quite. For backup, the authors relied on Egginton's widow, Brenda, who proved to be a veritable fount of venom where Dr. Wilson was concerned. Shown a photo of the surgeon, she declared, "That's a young looking one, he was very much fatter than that...fatter in the face and black eyes. He looks a lot younger there than he ever looked to me."[96]

Old, fat face aside, Brenda Egginton went on: "Although quite bright, he was a most objectionable person...rude, aggressive, unpleasant...bumptious...bossy...nasty....[H]e had a sense of humor in a nasty way...his language was filthy...and he drank an awful lot. He had more than a bob on himself."[97] The ellipses are Martin's and Boyd's, leaving readers to wonder what other posthumous insults, if any, they chose to omit.

Major Egginton's second letter to Witchell had asked that his statements on Wilson be kept confidential "in deference to the memory of a man I liked." Apprised of those words, Brenda Egginton fumed, "He didn't say he liked him. I didn't know that he liked him, but obviously he did, if he said he did. Well that was all right by me, it was up to him what he did. I didn't like him, the young wives didn't like him...we were all anti-him, most of us anyway. He had this bull terrier which would go for the troops. It was thoroughly unpleasant." Even the doctor's gardening offended Brenda: "He was definitely incompetent: he used to flatten everything—beautiful bushes and things like that."[98]

What of the photo-hoax confession? "I was told one evening when he had been drinking round the table," Brenda said. "We all laughed at him, we didn't believe him." Perhaps sensing her interviewers' disappointment, she quickly back-pedaled, saying, "Everybody knew, we knew up there. We all laughed about it, we have done so for years. We knew the story, my husband did, I did too. I find it incredible that the hoax lasted so long."[99]

So, did Brenda believe it, or not? Once again, Boyd and Martin were happy to have it both ways.

Almost as an afterthought, Martin and Boyd turned their minds to more substantive questions surrounding the two Wilson photos. Boyd claimed credit for rediscovering the uncropped version of the "swan-neck" photo in 1986, claiming that it had vanished after its initial publication in April 1934 and that "nobody was aware it existed." In fact, as we have seen, Steuart Campbell published the uncropped photo two years earlier, in his April 1984 article for the *British Journal of Photography*. Boyd could not have failed to notice, since that article appears among his own book's list of sources.[100]

How to explain the discrepancy between Ian Wetherell's "substantiated" account of snapping the photos with a Leica, versus Egginton's tale of an anonymous friend using a radically different technique? Martin and Boyd suggest that Maurice Chambers "was perhaps" the one who made the strange and pointless switch from film to quarter-plates, while Dr. Wilson "played out the rest."[101] Again, they contradict Ian's claim that Chambers sent the "strip of film" to be developed—and the best they can offer at that is "perhaps." Left hanging is the question as to *why* a change of film was necessary in the first place.

Regarding Wilson's second photo, of what seems to be a head submerging in the loch, Martin and Boyd note that "the image is poor and fuzzy, there is no background to give scale, and the shape of the head and the water texture are very different to that in the Surgeon's Photograph." They quote one Edgar Kingston—identified only as "an advocate of the Surgeon's Photograph"—who "bravely wrote," in 1962: "I think...that it is reasonably certain that the surgeon's two photographs must have been taken at different places and at different times."[102]

Not according to star witnesses Ian Wetherell and Christian Spurling, of course, but what prompted Kingston's opinion? He opines "beyond doubt that the second picture could not possibly have been taken immediately after the first...and that the indications are of a considerable time lapse between the two exposures." Based on what? He doesn't say, content to surmise that "the two pictures could be of two different objects."[103]

Indeed, they *could,* but it is Kingston's case to prove. He offers nothing in support of it.

While fumbling to explain why Spurling could not even state the year in which he helped his step-father concoct the photo hoax, Martin and Boyd reverted to the "so what/who cares?" defense. "Of course," they wrote, "the real danger is that one is being drawn into an academic exercise! The reality is that Wilson did *not* take the photograph and so the object was not photographed on the 21st of April 1934 [*sic*]. It could have been taken anytime between December 1933 and April of 1934, with all the extremes of weather these months would entail." (Emphasis in the original.)[104]

As usual, that "explanation" raises problems without solving any. No one has ever claimed Wilson's photos were snapped on 21 April 1934, the day one first appeared in print. And if the plot was carried out before mid-January 1934, Duke Wetherell could not have had the motive claimed by both his son and Christian Spurling—i.e., cooking up a prank that would humiliate the *Daily Mail.* His first hoax, with the hippo's foot, was not exposed in 1933, thus Wetherell had no sane reason to concoct a second fraud motivated by revenge.

It hardly mattered, though, as Boyd and Martin closed their slender book with self-congratulation. "The evidence we have presented in this booklet," they declared, "is irrefutable in its statement that the Surgeon's Photograph is a hoax....[C]an anyone suggest a more probable explanation than the one we have offered here, and in doing so, refute the validity of the Mandrake article? The challenge is laid open........!" [Final ellipsis in the original.][105]

Ironically, as demonstrated earlier, Martin and Boyd *themselves* refute that article's validity. If their story (and Spurling's) is correct, then Ian Wetherell was wrong about the camera used in 1934, the film employed, and the identity of the person who submitted the film for development. The only thing irrefutable about Spurling's tale is that it failed to solve a mystery.

References

1. "Loch Ness," Wikipedia, http://en.wikipedia.org/wiki/Loch_Ness.
2. Ronald Binns, "The Nessie and Other Lake Monsters Are the Products of Weak Minds," in *Lake Monsters: Fact of Fiction?*, Paul Shovlin editor (Detroit: Thomson Gale, 2005), p. 85.
3. Henry Bauer, *The Enigma of Loch Ness* (Stirling: Johnston & Bacon Books, 1991).
4. Binns, pp. 85-6.
5. Bauer, pp. 149-52.
6. "Classic Cases: The Spicers," Loch Ness Monster, http://lochnessmystery.blogspot.com/2010/08/classic-sightings-spicers.html.

7. Nicholas Witchell, *The Loch Ness Story* (London: Corgi, 1982), pp. 46-9; David Martin and Alastair Boyd, *Nessie: The Surgeon's Photograph Exposed* (East Barnet, Hertfordshire: The Authors, 1999), p. 22.

8. Martin and Boyd, p. 34; "M. A. Wetherell," IMDB, http://www.imdb.com/name/nm0923143.

9. Martin and Boyd, pp. 22-4; Witchell, p. 49.

10. Witchell, p. 49.

11. Ibid.; Martin and Boyd, p. 25.

12. Witchell, p. 51.

13. Ibid., p. 52; Martin and Boyd, pp. 28-9.

14. Martin and Boyd, pp. 25, 30-2.

15. Martin and Boyd, pp. 31-2; Witchell, p. 52.

16. Martin and Boyd, p. 33.

17. Ibid., 54-5; Witchell, pp. 54-5.

18. Roy Mackal, *The Monsters of Loch Ness* (Chicago: Swallow Press, 1976), p. 96; Witchell, p. 54.

19. Martin and Boyd, p. 56; Bauer, pp. 8, 11.

20. Tim Dinsdale, *Loch Ness Monster* 4th ed. (London: Routledge & Kegan Paul, 1982), p. 200; Mackal, *Monsters*, p. 96; Henry Bauer, "Common Knowledge about the Loch Ness Monster: Television, Videos, and Films," *Journal of Scientific Exploration*, Vol. 16, No. 3 (2002): 456, 460; Paul Harrison, *The Encyclopedia of the Loch Ness Monster* (London: Robert Hale, 1999), pp. 184, 203; John Kirk, "Another Point of View," The Shadowlands Sea Serpent Page, http://theshadowlands.net/hoax.htm.

21. Steuart Campbell, *The Loch Ness Monster: The Evidence* rev. ed. (Aberdeen: Aberdeen University Press, 1991), p. 36; Witchell, p. 54.

22. Martin and Boyd, pp. 56.

23. Dinsdale, pp. 57-8, 200-1.

24. Martin and Boyd, p. 83.

25. Witchell, pp. 156-7; Harrison, p. 32.

26. Witchell, p. 57.

27. Bauer, "Common Knowledge," p. 460.

28. The Loch Ness Underwater Photographic Evidence, http://www.loch-ness.org/underwaterpictures.html.

29. Mackal, *Monsters*, p. 98.

30. Mangiacopra and Smith, *Does Champ Exist?*, pp. 107-8.

31. Binns, pp. 83-92.

32. Ibid., pp. 88-9.

33. Ibid., p. 82.

34. Elizabeth Campbell and David Solomon, *The Search for Morag* (New York: Walker and Company, 1973), pp. 151-2.

35. Bauer, *Enigma*, p. 55.

36. Adrian Shine, review of *The Loch Ness Mystery Solved*, in *Cryptozoology* 4 (1985): 83.

37. Ibid., p. 85.

38. Ibid., pp. 85-6.

39. Ibid., p. 86.

40. Ibid., p. 85.

41. Ibid.

42. Ibid., pp. 85-6.

43. Steuart Campbell, http://www.steuartcampbell.com; "Steuart Campbell," Wikipedia, http://en.wikipedia.org/wiki/Steuart_Campbell.

44. Steuart Campbell, "The Surgeon's Monster Hoax," *British Journal of Photography* Vol. 131, No. 6454 (20 April 1984): 407-411.

45. Campbell, *The Loch Ness Monster*, p. 38.

46. Paul LeBlond and Michael Collins, "The Wilson Nessie Photo: A Size Determination Based on Physical Principles," *Cryptozoology* 6 (1987): 55-64.

47. Roy Mackal, "The Wilson Photo: Bird Explanation Now Untenable," *Cryptozoology* 7 (1988): 115.

48. Steuart Campbell, "The Tail of an Otter?" *Cryptozoology* 7 (1988): 116-17; Paul LeBlond, "The Tail of an Otter?" *Cryptozoology* 7 (1988): 117-18; Steuart Campbell, "Disinherit the Wind," *Cryptozoology* 8 (1989): 129-32; Paul LeBlond, "Whence Blew the Wind?" *Cryptozoology* 8 (1989): 133-5.

49. "Making of a monster," *Sunday Telegraph,* 7 December 1975.

50. Ibid.

51. Bauer, *Enigma*, pp. 153-6.

52. Ronald Binns, *The Loch Ness Mystery Solved* (London: W. H. Allen, 1984), p. 97.

53. Martin and Boyd, p. 58.

54. Dinsdale, p. 201.

55. Martin and Boyd, p. 58.

56. Ibid., pp. 13, 15-16, 19-20, 40.

57. Ibid., pp. 40-2.

58. Ibid., pp. 19-20, back cover; Harrison, pp. 27-8.

59. Martin and Boyd, pp. 43-6.

60. Ibid., p. 4.

61. Ibid., pp. 42, 81.

62. John Darnton, "Loch Ness: Fiction Is Stranger Than Truth," *New York Times,* 20 March 1994.

63. "Fake in the Lake," *People* Vo. 41, No. 11, 28 March 1994.

64. Karl Shuker, *In Search of Prehistoric Survivors* (London: Blandford Press, 1995), p. 87; Martin and Boyd, p. 43.

65. Martin and Boyd, p. 45.

66. Richard Smith, "The Classic Wilson Nessie Photo: Is the Hoax a Hoax?" *Fate*, 48, No. 11 (November 1995): 42–44.

67. Joe Nickell, "Nessie Hoax Redux," *Skeptical Inquirer* 6 (March 1996), http://www.csicop.org/sb/show/nessie_hoax_redux.

68. Michael Newton, "Florida Sea Monster Revisited," *Fate* 61 (March 2008).

69. Nickell, "Nessie Hoax Redux."

70. Ibid.

71. Ibid.

72. Ibid.

73. Ibid.

74. Ibid.

75. Ibid.

76. Ibid.; Campbell, *The Loch Ness Monster,* pp. 55-64.

77. Radford and Nickell, *Lake Monster Mysteries,* pp. 17-19.

78. Nickell, "Nessie Hoax Redux."

79. Joe Nickell, " Nessie Hoax Redux II," *Skeptical Inquirer* 6 (September 1996), http://www.csicop.org/sb/show/nessie_hoax_redux_ii.

80. Bauer, "Common Knowledge," p. 468; Martin and Boyd, p. 60.

81. "Rival Loch Ness Monster centres resolve name row," BBC News, 30 June 2010.

82. Martin and Boyd, pp. 54-5.

83. Ibid., pp. 59-60.

84. Ibid., pp. 57-8, 62-6.

85. Ibid., p 60

86. Ibid., p. 70.

87. Ibid., p. 67.

87. Ibid., p. 70.

88. Ibid.

89. Ibid.

90. Ibid.

91. Ibid.

92. Ibid., pp. 74-5.

93. Ibid., pp. 68-9.

94. Ibid., p. 71.

95. Ibid., p. 73.

96. Ibid., p. 76.

97. Ibid.

98. Ibid., pp. 73, 76-7.

99. Ibid., pp. 77-8.

100. Ibid., pp. 93, 98; Campbell, "The Surgeon's Monster Hoax."

101. Martin and Boyd, p. 92

102. Ibid., pp. 87-8.

103. Ibid., pp. 88-9.

104. Ibid., p. 84.

In Conclusion

The cases we've examined in preceding chapters are diverse, running the gamut of purported evidence and skeptical response. In each, however, we discern a certain commonality.

The first case, St. Augustine's globster, offered a massive and potentially unique physical specimen, beached for weeks (at least) and readily available for scientific study. Sadly, none occurred, and the chief contemporary expert who dismissed it as a "sick whale's nose" never came within 900 miles of the carcass. Later study of the creature's tissue suggested a giant mollusk. Debunkers of that proposition published two reports, nine years apart, flatly contradicting themselves without explaining the discrepancy.

Another case, Florida's "Three-Toes," served up secondary evidence in the form of numerous footprints. Some of those were studied *in situ* by a qualified zoologist and engineers who documented their conclusions. That report, in turn, was totally ignored by mainstream journalists in 1948, and again four decades later, as they rushed to rubber-stamp a hoax confession riddled with more holes than the average slice of Swiss cheese. In the process, one self-styled investigative reporter saw fit to posthumously slander the original investigator of the tracks, dismissing his sterling academic credentials to call him a "self-taught zoologist."

Hoaxer Raymond Wallace left behind some photographs of hand-carved "Sasquatch feet," but no other substantive evidence beyond his worthless word—or, rather, that of his survivors, bent on banking cash advances for the film rights to his story—yet the media ignored his history of pathological deception, verging on dementia, to crown him as the "inventor" of a "legend" known worldwide for centuries before his birth.

Our three remaining cases hinge on photographs or motion-picture film. Any or all of them *may* be fakes, but in their zeal to prove as much, professional debunkers have relied exclusively on hearsay evidence, replete with baseless speculation, fatal contradictions, fabrication, and improbabilities that make some claims from Bigfoot-Nessie witnesses seem positively mundane by comparison. When caught red-handed at it, the "investigators" shrug their problems off as routine "skeptical" thinking.

Nothing could be further from the truth.

True skeptics absolutely question claims of paranormal happenings, but they are open to examining such evidence as may exist, evaluating it on rational, coherent grounds, without resort to ridicule, concoction of bizarre hypotheses, and other tactics that identify a "true believer." Or, in this case, a committed *un*believer. They do not insist, like Ronald Binns, that all purported Nessie photos *must* be fakes, then fabricate a rationale for that prejudged conclusion.

Separating skofftics from true skeptics is not difficult. The former, while pretending to be open-minded and denying any bias on a given subject, constantly resort to fallacious arguments—which they, of course, are quick to note and criticize if used by those they criticize. Some of those fallacies include:

- Errors of fact, which may suggest poor research or—in the worst-case scenario—outright deception. Clearly, there is no truth to the claim that Ray Wallace "invented" Bigfoot in 1958, nor even pioneered hoaxed footprints in that year, when mentor Rant Mullens began faking tracks a quarter-century earlier. Published references to a "giant penguin panic" in Florida's 1948 "Three-Toes" case are likewise nonsensical, when no penguin of any size was proposed as a suspect prior to 1968.
- Employment of double standards. Strident denials notwithstanding, this technique is *de rigueur* for skofftics. Lapses in a subject's memory, occasioned by the passage of a quarter-century or more, brand any witness to a cryptid sighting as a liar, while abundant errors in a hoax "confession" are dismissed as normal. Likewise, if a witness to some extraordinary incident delays reporting it, they are considered unreliable, but the confession of a hoax, postponed for sixty years, is instantly accepted—even when that long delay defeats the purpose of the prank, as in the case of Dr. Wilson's Loch Ness photos.
- Inconsistency or contradiction, with discrepancies ignored and unexplained. In their analysis of various globsters, Sidney Pierce and his coauthors first identified the Bermuda carcass as a cold-blooded vertebrate (1995), then as whale blubber (2004), citing the first report in support of the second. Kal Korff first named Jerry Romney as Roger Patterson's "man in the ape suit," then switched to Bob Heironimus without explaining his apparent error. David Martin and Alastair Boyd present two contradictory accounts of how the Wilson photo was produced, while seeming to suggest that *both* are simultaneously true.
- *Ad hominem* attacks, targeting "the person" rather than objective fact, include Greg Long's posthumous character assassination of Roger Patterson and his near-hysterical email assaults on living critics of his work; the slightly more restrained attack on Dr. Wilson's character by David Martin and Alastair Boyd; Jeff Klinkenberg's misrepresentation of Ivan Sanderson as "a self-taught zoologist"; and the snide claim from Ben Radford and Joe Nickell that "middle-aged Vermont women" are somehow prone to seeing nonexistent creatures.

- Circular reasoning is presented most blatantly in the work of Ronald Binns and Mark Chorvinsky. Binns, assuming that all purported photos of Nessie are "fakes and/or models," dictates that they must be staged near shore. Thus, when a specific snapshot—like the Wilson photo—shows no foreground whatsoever, Binns feels justified in claiming that "the object shown...is very close to shore," and therefore is "suspicious." In Chorvinsky's case, fearing John Chambers would deny making a Sasquatch costume for the Patterson film, the author shunned his best possible source in favor of "tracking down rumors," then supported that odd approach by quoting a third party, admittedly ignorant of the facts, who surmised that "the secret will die with [Chambers]." That shoddy tactic served double duty when Chambers himself denied participation in the filming—proof positive, to Chorvinsky, that Chambers was lying!

- Appeals to ridicule are sadly common in skofftic writings, as when Greg Long mocks the accents and appearance of subjects he has interviewed, or when the Radford-Nickell team describes the considered opinions of expert opponents as "comical." Ronald Binns, likewise, finds the opinions of his former colleagues—views that he once personally shared—"absurd and comical."

- Use of bad analogies attempts to persuade by misdirection. In his book "solving" the Loch Ness mystery, Ronald Binns flounders in his effort to explain how sonar operates, then compensates by veering off into an irrelevant discourse on "Piltdown Man," a hoax from 1912 wherein British geologist Charles Dawson presented bone fragments recovered from a gravel pit as remains of a previously unknown early human. *Time* magazine exposed the fraud in 1953, with experts declaring that the relics actually came from three different species. Presumably, if England spawned one hoax, its Scottish neighbors must be guilty of another.

- Appeals to authority are deemed fallacious when the source in question is not a legitimate authority on the subject. A prime example is Joe Nickell's reliance on Ronald Binns for "expert opinions" to dispute comments on trick photography from professional filmmaker Richard D. Smith. Binns, an embittered former monster-hunter, then accommodates Nickell by dismissing Smith's reasoned criticism of the Spurling hoax confession with vague "maybes," signifying nothing.

- The related tactic of appeals to *anonymous* authority is even more egregious, as with Greg Long's barroom interviews concerning Roger Patterson and the various unnamed "friends" of Dr. Wilson who allegedly "always knew" that his Loch Ness photos were fakes.

- Argument by repetition sometimes verges on the comical. Joe Nickell provides a classic—and rather ironic—example in his dismissive treatment of Richard Smith and the Wilson photo, when he writes: "The points Smith raises range from the untrue to the dubious, as we have seen, and he is merely repeating himself. In response, I will repeat again...." No double standard there!

- Guilt by association may be pernicious, as when Joe Nickell attacks Richard Smith for selling an article to *Fate* magazine, then implies that Smith somehow controlled placement of said article "sandwiched between" pieces by other authors, which Nickell deems to be ridiculous. Carried to an absurd degree, we might also include, once more, the Radford-Nickell suggestion that middle-aged Vermont women are somehow more prone to see lake monsters than are their younger, male neighbors.

- The "straw man" fallacy, debunking claims raised by no one, is exemplified by author Mike Dash's handling of the Florida "Three-Toes" case. After referring to a nonexistent "giant penguin panic," Dash suggests that various witnesses who described unidentified creatures—none of them even vaguely resembling a penguin—either lied outright or altered their accounts to please interrogators (who, in turn, were asked nothing about penguins). Ben Radford tried a similar trick at Lake Champlain, confidently stating that "a single monster can neither live for centuries nor reproduce itself." Needless to say, no serious researcher ever claimed any such thing.

- Argument by selective observation, otherwise known as "cherry-picking," is another common tactic. David Martin and Alastair Boyd offer a clear example, lifting one sentence from a letter written a relative of Dr. Wilson to suggest that various family members thought him a hoaxer. Read in its entirety, the letter presents a very different picture, even questioning the motives of the youth who thought his father faked the famous Loch Ness photograph.

- Shifting the burden of proof is particularly dishonest. Skofftics are fond of quoting the maxim that "extraordinary claims require extraordinary proof," generally credited to CSICOP founder Marcello Truzzi (or, alternatively, to Carl Sagan). Though perfectly sound in itself, that mantra rings hollow when professional debunkers float theories devoid of supporting evidence, while demanding that their critics prove a negative in order to refute them. Ben Radford sculpts a mini-log from clay, identical in form to the much larger object in Sandra Mansi's "Champ" photo, and pronounces the mystery solved, writing: "I cannot conclusively prove the object is a tree; fortunately, I don't have to." In the same vein, David Martin and Alastair Boyd pronounce their mutually contradictory accounts of Dr. Wilson's photo "irrefutable," then close by asking, "Can anyone suggest a more probable explanation than the one we have offered here, and in doing so, refute the validity of the Mandrake article? The challenge is laid open........!"

Such tactics make a mockery of honest skepticism and belie Greg Long's defense of partner Kal Korff, implicitly extended here to his compatriots, insisting that "he's NOT A DEBUNKER IN THE SENSE of A CLOSE-MINDED SKEPTIC." Clearly, some of those encountered in preceding chapters *are* closed-minded, seeking facts to buttress preconceived rejections of specific evidence or a phenomenon in general, and making due with speculation when they find no evidence. Others, while seeming well-intentioned, would appear to be confused, as when they cite findings from one document in support of a second, contradictory report.

As for the mainstream media—dubbed "lamestream" by failed Alaska governor and far-right Fox "News" propagandist Sarah Palin—its representatives too often seem to choose the path of least resistance, demonstrating a propensity to swallow fabricated tales and spit them out again with colorful "embellishments" that take them even further from objective fact. If nothing else, the cases documented here suggest that persons interested in the truth should take nothing for granted, even when it wears the "skeptic" brand.

About the Author

Michael Newton has published 274 books since 1977, with 9 more scheduled for release from various houses through 2014. His works in the field of cryptozoology include *Monsters, Mysteries and Man* (1979); *The Encyclopedia of Cryptozoology* (2005; ranked as one of twelve "Outstanding Reference Books" by the American Library Association); *Strange Indiana Monsters* (2006); *Florida's Unexpected Wildlife* (2007); *Hidden Animals* (2009); *Giant Snakes* (2009); *Strange California Monsters* (2009); *Strange Kentucky Monsters* (2009); *Strange Monsters of the Pacific Northwest* (2011); *When Bigfoot Attacks* (2011); *Strange Pennsylvania Monsters* (2012); *Hopsquatch* (a novel, 2012); and *Globsters* (2012).

STILL ON THE TRACK OF UNKNOWN ANIMALS

The Centre for Fortean Zoology, or CFZ, is a non profit-making organisation founded in 1992 with the aim of being a clearing house for information, and coordinating research into mystery animals around the world.

We also study out of place animals, rare and aberrant animal behaviour, and Zooform Phenomena; little-understood "things" that appear to be animals, but which are in fact nothing of the sort, and not even alive (at least in the way we understand the term).

Not only are we the biggest organisation of our type in the world, but - or so we like to think - we are the best. We are certainly the only truly global cryptozoological research organisation, and we carry out our investigations using a strictly scientific set of guidelines. We are expanding all the time and looking to recruit new members to help us in our research into mysterious animals and strange creatures across the globe.

Why should you join us? Because, if you are genuinely interested in trying to solve the last great mysteries of Mother Nature, there is nobody better than us with whom to do it.

Members get a four-issue subscription to our journal *Animals & Men.* Each issue contains nearly 100 pages packed with news, articles, letters, research papers, field reports, and even a gossip column! The magazine is Royal Octavo in format with a full colour cover. You also have access to one of the world's largest collections of resource material dealing with cryptozoology and allied disciplines, and people from the CFZ membership regularly take part in fieldwork and expeditions around the world.

The CFZ is managed by a three-man board of trustees, with a non-profit making trust registered with HM Government Stamp Office. The board of trustees is supported by a Permanent Directorate of full and part-time staff, and advised by a Consultancy Board of specialists - many of whom are world-renowned experts in their particular field. We have regional representatives across the UK, the USA, and many other parts of the world, and are affiliated with

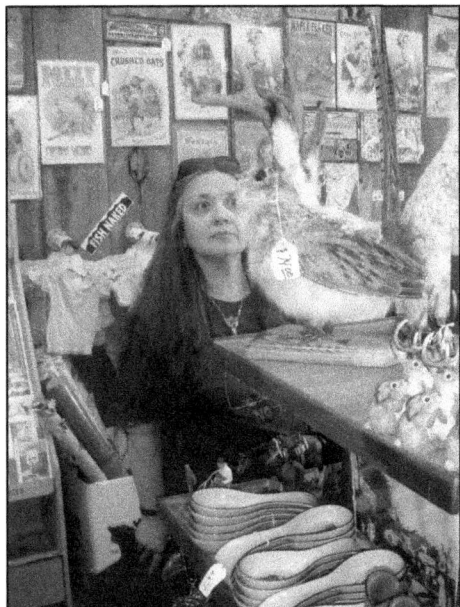

You'll find that the people at the CFZ are friendly and approachable. We have a thriving forum on the website which is the hub of an ever-growing electronic community. You will soon find your feet. Many members of the CFZ Permanent Directorate started off as ordinary members, and now work full-time chasing monsters around the world.

Write to us, e-mail us, or telephone us. The list of future projects on the website is not exhaustive. If you have a good idea for an investigation, please tell us. We may well be able to help.

We are always looking for volunteers to join us. If you see a project that interests you, do not hesitate to get in touch with us. Under certain circumstances we can help provide funding for your trip. If you look on the future projects section of the website, you can see some of the projects that we have pencilled in for the next few years.

In 2003 and 2004 we sent three-man expeditions to Sumatra looking for Orang-Pendek - a semi-legendary bipedal ape. The same three went to Mongolia in 2005. All three members started off merely subscribers to the CFZ magazine. Next time it could be you!

We have no magic sources of income. All our funds come from donations, membership fees, and sales of our publications and merchandise. We are always looking for corporate sponsorship, and other sources of revenue. If you have any ideas for fund-raising please let us know. However, unlike other cryptozoological organisations in the past, we do not live in an intellectual ivory tower. We are not afraid to get our hands dirty, and furthermore we are not one of those organisations where the membership have to raise money so that a privileged few can go on expensive foreign trips. Our research teams, both in the UK and abroad, consist of a mixture of experienced and inexperienced personnel. We are truly a community, and work on the premise that the benefits of CFZ membership are open to all.

Reports of our investigations are published on our website as soon as they are available. Preliminary reports are posted within days of the project finishing.

Each year we publish a 200 page yearbook

We have a thriving YouTube channel, CFZtv, which has well over two hundred self-made documentaries, lecture appearances, and episodes of our monthly webTV show. We have a daily online magazine, which has over a million hits each year.

Each year since 2000 we have held our annual convention - the Weird Weekend. It is three days of lectures, workshops, and excursions. But most importantly it is a chance for members of the CFZ to meet each other, and to talk with the members of the permanent directorate in a relaxed and informal setting and preferably with a pint of beer in one hand. Since 2006 - the Weird Weekend has been bigger and better and held on the third weekend in August in the idyllic rural location of Woolsery in North Devon.

Since relocating to North Devon in 2005 we have become ever more closely involved with other community organisations, and we hope that this trend will continue. We have also worked closely with Police Forces across the UK as consultants for animal mutilation cases, and we intend to forge closer links with the coastguard and other community services. We want to work closely with those who regularly travel into the Bristol Channel, so that if the recent trend of exotic animal visitors to our coastal waters continues, we can be out there as soon as possible.

© UndergroundImages2007

Apart from having been the only Fortean Zoological organisation in the world to have consistently published material on all aspects of the subject for over a decade, we have achieved the following concrete results:

• Disproved the myth relating to the headless so-called sea-serpent carcass of Durgan beach in Cornwall 1975

• Disproved the story

- of the 1988 puma skull of Lustleigh Cleave
- Carried out the only in-depth research ever into the mythos of the Cornish Owlman.
- Made the first records of a tropical species of lamprey
- Made the first records of a luminous cave gnat larva in Thailand
- Discovered a possible new species of British mammal - the beech marten
- In 1994-6 carried out the first archival fortean zoological survey of Hong Kong
- In the year 2000, CFZ theories were confirmed when a new species of lizard was added to the British List
- Identified the monster of Martin Mere in Lancashire as a giant wels catfish
- Expanded the known range of Armitage's skink in the Gambia by 80%
- Obtained photographic evidence of the remains of Europe's largest known pike
- Carried out the first ever in-depth study of the ninki-nanka
- Carried out the first attempt to breed Puerto Rican cave snails in captivity

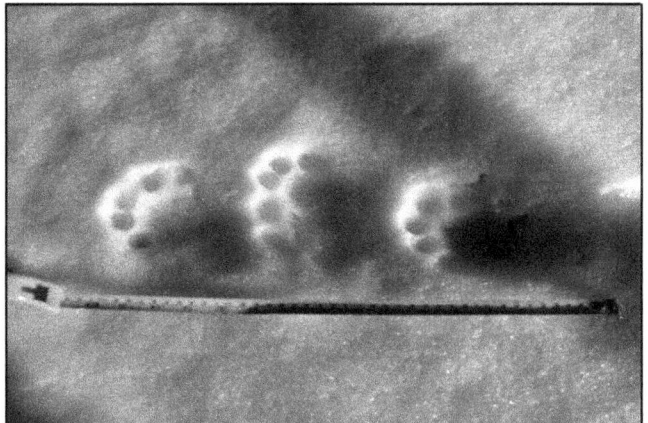

- Were the first European explorers to visit the `lost valley` in Sumatra
- Published the first ever evidence for a new tribe of pygmies in Guyana
- Published the first evidence for a new species of caiman in Guyana

on a monster-haunted lake in Ireland for the first time

- Had a sighting of orang pendek in Sumatra in 2009
- Found leopard hair, subsequently identified by DNA analysis, from rural North Devon in 2010
- Brought back hairs which appear to be from an unknown primate in Sumatra
- Published some of the best evidence ever for the almasty in southern Russia

CFZ Expeditions and Investigations include:

- 1998 Puerto Rico, Florida, Mexico (Chupacabras)
- 1999 Nevada (Bigfoot)
- 2000 Thailand (Naga)
- 2002 Martin Mere (Giant catfish)
- 2002 Cleveland (Wallaby mutilation)
- 2003 Bolam Lake (BHM Reports)

- 2003 Sumatra (Orang Pendek)
- 2003 Texas (Bigfoot; giant snapping turtles)
- 2004 Sumatra (Orang Pendek; cigau, a sabre-toothed cat)
- 2004 Illinois (Black panthers; cicada swarm)
- 2004 Texas (Mystery blue dog)
- Loch Morar (Monster)
- 2004 Puerto Rico (Chupacabras; carnivorous cave snails)
- 2005 Belize (Affiliate expedition for hairy dwarfs)
- 2005 Loch Ness (Monster)
- 2005 Mongolia (Allghoi Khorkhoi aka Mongolian death worm)

- 2006 Gambia (Gambo - Gambian sea monster , Ninki Nanka and Armitage's skink
- 2006 Llangorse Lake (Giant pike, giant eels)
- 2006 Windermere (Giant eels)
- 2007 Coniston Water (Giant eels)
- 2007 Guyana (Giant anaconda, didi, water tiger)
- 2008 Russia (Almasty)
- 2009 Sumatra (Orang pendek)
- 2009 Republic of Ireland (Lake Monster)
- 2010 Texas (Blue Dogs)
- 2010 India (Mande Burung)
- 2011 Sumatra (Orang-pendek)

For details of current membership fees, current expeditions and investigations, and voluntary posts within the CFZ that need your help, please do not hesitate to contact us.

The Centre for Fortean Zoology,
Myrtle Cottage,
Woolfardisworthy,
Bideford, North Devon
EX39 5QR

Telephone 01237 431413
Fax+44 (0)7006-074-925
eMail info@cfz.org.uk

Websites:

www.cfz.org.uk
www.weirdweekend.org

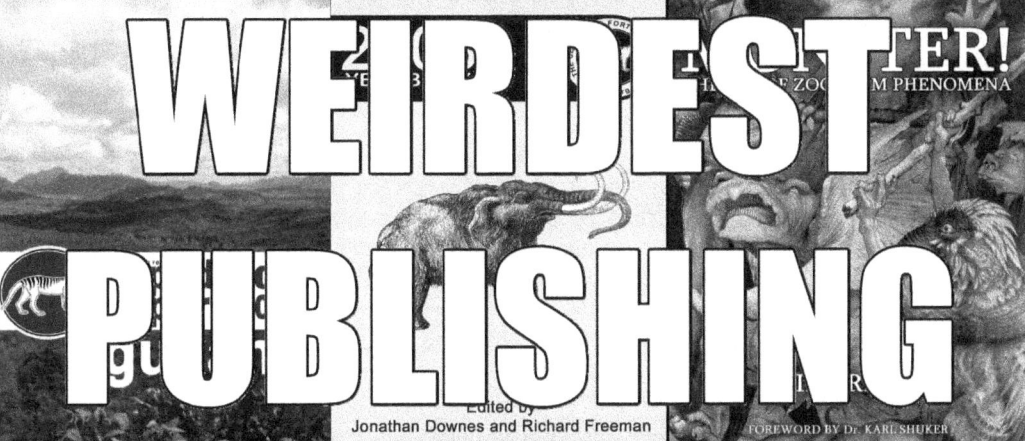

THE WORLD'S WEIRDEST PUBLISHING COMPANY

HOW TO START A PUBLISHING EMPIRE

Unlike most mainstream publishers, we have a non-commercial remit, and our mission statement claims that "we publish books because they deserve to be published, not because we think that we can make money out of them". Our motto is the Latin Tag *Pro bona causa facimus* (we do it for good reason), a slogan taken from a children's book *The Case of the Silver Egg* by the late Desmond Skirrow.

WIKIPEDIA: "The first book published was in 1988. *Take this Brother may it Serve you Well* was a guide to Beatles bootlegs by Jonathan Downes. It sold quite well, but was hampered by very poor production values, being photocopied, and held together by a plastic clip binder. In 1988 A5 clip binders were hard to get hold of, so the publishers took A4 binders and cut them in half with a hacksaw. It now reaches surprisingly high prices second hand.

The production quality improved slightly over the years, and after 1999 all the books produced were ringbound with laminated colour covers. In 2004, however, they signed an agreement with Lightning Source, and all books are now produced perfect bound, with full colour covers."

Until 2010 all our books, the majority of which are/were on the subject of mystery animals and allied disciplines, were published by `CFZ Press`, the publishing arm of the Centre for Fortean Zoology (CFZ), and we urged our readers and followers to draw a discreet veil over the books that we published that were completely off topic to the CFZ.

However, in 2010 we decided that enough was enough and launched a second imprint, `Fortean Words` which aims to cover a wide range of non animal-related esoteric subjects. Other imprints will be launched as and when we feel like it, however the basic ethos of the company remains the same: Our job is to publish books and magazines that we feel are worth publishing, whether or not they are going to sell. Money is, after all - as my dear old Mama once told me - a rather vulgar subject, and she would be rolling in her grave if she thought that her eldest son was somehow in `trade`.

Luckily, so far our tastes have turned out not to be that rarified after all, and we have sold far more books than anyone ever thought that we would, so there is a moral in there somewhere…

Jon Downes,
Woolsery, North Devon
July 2010

CFZ PRESS

Other Books in Print

Wildman! by Redfern, Nick
Globsters by Newton, Michael
Cats of Magic, Mythology and Mystery Shuker, by Karl P. N
Those Amazing Newfoundland Dogs by Bondeson, Jan
The Mystery Animals of Pennsylvania by Gable, Andrew
Sea Serpent Carcasses - Scotland from the Stronsa Monster to Loch Ness by Glen Vaudrey
The CFZ Yearbook 2012 edited by Jonathan and Corinna Downes
ORANG PENDEK: Sumatra's Forgotten Ape by Richard Freeman
THE MYSTERY ANIMALS OF THE BRITISH ISLES: London by Neil Arnold
CFZ EXPEDITION REPORT: India 2010 by Richard Freeman *et al*
The Cryptid Creatures of Florida by Scott Marlow
Dead of Night by Lee Walker
The Mystery Animals of the British Isles: The Northern Isles by Glen Vaudrey
THE MYSTERY ANIMALS OF THE BRTISH ISLES: Gloucestershire and Worcestershire by
Paul Williams
When Bigfoot Attacks by Michael Newton
Weird Waters – The Mystery Animals of Scandinavia: Lake and Sea Monsters by Lars Thomas
The Inhumanoids by Barton Nunnelly
Monstrum! A Wizard's Tale by Tony "Doc" Shiels
CFZ Yearbook 2011 edited by Jonathan Downes
Karl Shuker's Alien Zoo by Shuker, Dr Karl P.N
Tetrapod Zoology Book One by Naish, Dr Darren
The Mystery Animals of Ireland by Gary Cunningham and Ronan Coghlan
Monsters of Texas by Gerhard, Ken
The Great Yokai Encyclopaedia by Freeman, Richard
NEW HORIZONS: Animals & Men issues 16-20 Collected Editions Vol. 4
by Downes, Jonathan
A Daintree Diary -
Tales from Travels to the Daintree Rainforest in tropical north Queensland, Australia
by Portman, Carl
Strangely Strange but Oddly Normal by Roberts, Andy

by Downes, Jonathan
The Smaller Mystery Carnivores of the Westcountry by Downes, Jonathan
CFZ EXPEDITION REPORT: Gambia 2006 by Richard Freeman *et al*, Shuker, Karl (fwd)
The Owlman and Others by Jonathan Downes
The Blackdown Mystery by Downes, Jonathan
Big Cats in Britain Yearbook 2006 by Fraser, Mark (Ed)
Fragrant Harbours - Distant Rivers by Downes, John T
Only Fools and Goatsuckers by Downes, Jonathan
Monster of the Mere by Jonathan Downes
Dragons:More than a Myth by Freeman, Richard Alan
Granfer's Bible Stories by Downes, John Tweddell
Monster Hunter by Downes, Jonathan

CFZ Classics is a new venture for us. There are many seminal works that are either unavailable today, or not available with the production values which we would like to see. So, following the old adage that if you want to get something done do it yourself, this is exactly what we have done.

Desiderius Erasmus Roterodamus (b. October 18th 1466, d. July 2nd 1536) said: "When I have a little money, I buy books; and if I have any left, I buy food and clothes," and we are much the same. Only, we are in the lucky position of being able to share our books with the wider world. CFZ Classics is a conduit through which we cannot just re-issue titles which we feel still have much to offer the cryptozoological and Fortean research communities of the 21st Century, but we are adding footnotes, supplementary essays, and other material where we deem it appropriate.

Headhunters of The Amazon by Fritz W Up de Graff (1902)

Fortean Words

The Centre for Fortean Zoology has for several years led the field in Fortean publishing. CFZ Press is the only publishing company specialising in books on monsters and mystery animals. CFZ Press has published more books on this subject than any other company in history and has attracted such well known authors as Andy Roberts, Nick Redfern, Michael Newton, Dr Karl Shuker, Neil Arnold, Dr Darren Naish, Jon Downes, Ken Gerhard and Richard Freeman.

Now CFZ Press are launching a new imprint. Fortean Words is a new line of books dealing with Fortean subjects other than cryptozoology, which is - after all - the subject the CFZ are best known for. Fortean Words is being launched with a spectacular multi-volume series called *Haunted Skies* which covers British UFO sightings between 1940 and 2010. Former policeman John Hanson and his long-suffering partner Dawn Holloway have compiled a peerless library of sighting reports, many that have not been made public before.

Other books include a look at the Berwyn Mountains UFO case by renowned Fortean Andy Roberts and a series of forthcoming books by transatlantic researcher Nick Redfern. CFZ Press are dedicated to maintaining the fine quality of their works with Fortean Words. New authors tackling new subjects will always be encouraged, and we hope that our books will continue to be as ground-breaking and popular as ever.

Haunted Skies Volume One 1940-1959 by John Hanson and Dawn Holloway
Haunted Skies Volume Two 1960-1965 by John Hanson and Dawn Holloway
Haunted Skies Volume Three 1965-1967 by John Hanson and Dawn Holloway
Haunted Skies Volume Four 1968-1971 by John Hanson and Dawn Holloway
Haunted Skies Volume Five 1972-1974 by John Hanson and Dawn Holloway
Haunted Skies Volume Six 1975-1977 by John Hanson and Dawn Holloway
Grave Concerns by Kai Roberts

Police and the Paranormal by Andy Owens
Dead of Night by Lee Walker
Space Girl Dead on Spaghetti Junction - an anthology by Nick Redfern
I Fort the Lore - an anthology by Paul Screeton
UFO Down - the Berwyn Mountains UFO Crash by Andy Roberts
The Grail by Ronan Coghlan
UFO Warminster - Cradle of Contract by Kevin Goodman
Quest for the Hexham Heads by Paul Screeton

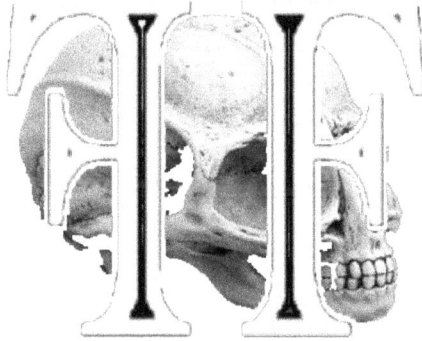

Fortean Fiction

Just before Christmas 2011, we launched our third imprint, this time dedicated to - let's see if you guessed it from the title - fictional books with a Fortean or cryptozoological theme. We have published a few fictional books in the past, but now think that because of our rising reputation as publishers of quality Forteana, that a dedicated fiction imprint was the order of the day.

We launched with four titles:

Green Unpleasant Land by Richard Freeman
Left Behind by Harriet Wadham
Dark Ness by Tabitca Cope
Snap! By Steven Bredice
Death on Dartmoor by Di Francis
Dark Wear by Tabitca Cope
Hyakymonogatari Book 1 by Richard Freeman

www.ingramcontent.com/pod-product-compliance
Lightning Source LLC
Chambersburg PA
CBHW051429090426
42737CB00014B/2879